Nature Bonds: Advancing Sustainable Finance by Supporting Biodiversity Conservation, Ecosystem Restoration, Climate Resilience, Green Investments, and Environmental Protection

Copyright

Nature Bonds: Advancing Sustainable Finance by Supporting Biodiversity Conservation, Ecosystem Restoration, Climate Resilience, Green Investments, and Environmental Protection

ISBN (eBook): 978-1-991368-31-7

ISBN (Paperback): 978-1-991368-32-4

Published by Global Climate Solutions

First Edition, 2025

Cover design and interior layout by Global Climate Solutions

Table of Contents

Introduction

Nature bonds represent a significant evolution in the intersection of finance and environmental stewardship. As global ecosystems face mounting pressures from climate change, biodiversity loss, and resource depletion, traditional funding mechanisms have proven inadequate to address the scale of investment required for sustainable solutions. Nature bonds emerge as an innovative financial instrument designed to channel capital directly into activities that conserve, restore, and enhance natural systems. They are structured debt instruments where repayment terms are often linked to achieving measurable environmental outcomes, thereby aligning investor interests with ecological priorities.

The rise of nature bonds reflects broader shifts in the financial sector toward sustainability. Investors are increasingly demanding products that deliver not only financial returns but also demonstrable social and environmental value. This demand is underpinned by the recognition that long-term financial stability cannot be separated from the health of ecosystems and the resilience of societies. By embedding accountability and performance metrics tied to conservation goals, nature bonds help bridge the gap between ecological needs and financial markets. They provide a mechanism for mobilizing private capital to complement limited public and philanthropic resources, offering a scalable pathway for addressing global environmental challenges.

At their core, nature bonds differ from conventional green bonds by focusing more explicitly on biodiversity, ecosystem services, and the protection of natural capital. While green bonds have often emphasized renewable energy or energy efficiency, nature bonds expand the scope of sustainable finance to include forests, wetlands, rivers, oceans, and other ecosystems critical for planetary health. This evolution reflects a growing awareness that tackling climate change and achieving sustainable development requires not only reducing emissions but also protecting and restoring the natural systems that regulate the global environment.

The promise of nature bonds lies in their ability to integrate ecological science with financial innovation. To be effective, these instruments must be supported by robust governance frameworks, credible monitoring and verification systems, and clear performance indicators. The environmental outcomes financed by nature bonds must be additional, measurable, and durable, ensuring that they deliver real impact rather than symbolic gestures. This demands collaboration across governments, financial institutions, international organizations, and local communities, all of whom play vital roles in designing, implementing, and overseeing these bonds.

Nature bonds also highlight the importance of inclusivity in sustainable finance. Conservation and climate initiatives often intersect with the livelihoods of communities who depend directly on natural resources. For nature bonds to succeed, they must incorporate mechanisms that ensure equitable benefits for these communities, respecting indigenous rights and promoting social as well as environmental outcomes. By doing so, they can foster greater legitimacy, resilience, and long-term sustainability.

This book situates nature bonds within the broader landscape of sustainable finance, exploring their foundations, structures, governance models, and potential to reshape global capital flows. It examines the challenges and opportunities inherent in scaling these instruments and situates them within international frameworks for climate and biodiversity action. Through this analysis, the book seeks to illuminate the pathways through which nature bonds can contribute to addressing some of the most pressing challenges of our time while advancing a vision of finance that works in harmony with nature.

Chapter 1: Foundations of Nature Bonds

Nature bonds are at the forefront of innovation in sustainable finance, designed to mobilize capital for biodiversity protection, ecosystem restoration, and climate resilience. Unlike traditional debt instruments, these bonds link financial performance to verifiable ecological outcomes, aligning investor returns with conservation goals. This chapter lays the groundwork for understanding their foundations by exploring the historical evolution of environmental finance, the conceptual underpinnings of nature-linked instruments, and the rationale for embedding natural capital into financial systems. By examining these elements, readers gain a clear framework for why nature bonds matter and how they can reshape global finance.

Origins and Conceptual Development

The concept of nature bonds originates from the broader evolution of sustainable finance, which has sought to reconcile the goals of capital markets with the imperatives of environmental and social well-being. In the early decades of environmental financing, most funding mechanisms were grant-based, reliant on multilateral institutions, development agencies, or philanthropic foundations. While such mechanisms provided essential seed capital, they lacked the scale and continuity needed to address global challenges such as biodiversity loss, climate change, and ecosystem degradation. The idea that financial markets themselves could be leveraged to address these crises gradually took hold, particularly during the early 2000s when green finance began to gain traction. Within this context, nature bonds emerged as a distinct class of instruments designed to channel investment into natural capital.

The intellectual foundations of nature bonds can be traced to the recognition of natural capital as an asset class. Natural capital refers to the world's stocks of natural resources, including soil, water, air, forests, and biodiversity, which collectively provide ecosystem services vital for human survival and economic prosperity.

Economists and policymakers increasingly acknowledged that the depletion of natural capital represented not only an ecological crisis but also a material financial risk. This reframing created the conditions for financial innovation that could monetize and safeguard ecosystem services. In essence, nature bonds were conceived as a mechanism for aligning financial returns with the preservation and restoration of natural systems, thereby internalizing environmental values into the logic of capital markets.

The development of green bonds laid the groundwork for nature bonds. Green bonds, first issued in the late 2000s by institutions such as the World Bank, were designed to raise funds specifically for climate and environmental projects. Their success demonstrated that investors were willing to accept instruments explicitly tied to sustainability outcomes. Over time, the green bond market expanded dramatically, attracting a diverse array of issuers, from sovereign governments to multinational corporations. However, while green bonds covered a wide spectrum of projects—ranging from renewable energy infrastructure to energy efficiency retrofits—they often lacked specific emphasis on biodiversity and ecosystems. This gap led to the conceptualization of nature bonds as instruments dedicated more directly to financing conservation, ecosystem restoration, and nature-based solutions.

Another important influence on the conceptual development of nature bonds was the debt-for-nature swap model that gained prominence in the 1980s and 1990s. Debt-for-nature swaps involved arrangements in which a portion of a developing country's external debt was forgiven in exchange for commitments to invest in conservation efforts. These swaps highlighted the potential for financial restructuring to deliver environmental outcomes, setting a precedent for the idea that debt instruments could be tied to ecological performance. However, debt-for-nature swaps were often limited in scope and faced challenges in implementation, including questions around monitoring and equitable distribution of benefits. Nonetheless, they provided a historical reference point for the evolution of more sophisticated instruments like nature bonds.

The broader policy environment also contributed to the conceptual development of nature bonds. International agreements such as the Paris Agreement and the Aichi Biodiversity Targets underscored the urgent need for financial flows to support conservation and climate action. These frameworks highlighted the multi-trillion-dollar gap between existing funding and what is required to achieve global sustainability objectives. Policymakers and financial actors alike began to search for scalable solutions that could mobilize private capital alongside public funding. Nature bonds were increasingly seen as a way to operationalize these goals, embedding biodiversity and ecosystem considerations directly into the structure of financial markets.

In addition to policy drivers, investor behavior played a critical role in shaping the conceptual development of nature bonds. The rapid growth of environmental, social, and governance (ESG) investing created demand for financial products that could credibly demonstrate positive environmental impact. Asset managers, pension funds, and sovereign wealth funds sought opportunities to diversify their portfolios while aligning with sustainability commitments. Nature bonds offered a mechanism to meet this demand, providing investors with measurable ecological outcomes tied to their investments. The integration of science-based targets and environmental performance metrics into bond structures further reinforced the credibility and attractiveness of these instruments.

Technological advancements also contributed to the origins of nature bonds. The development of remote sensing, satellite monitoring, and advanced data analytics enabled more accurate measurement and verification of environmental outcomes. These technologies addressed one of the long-standing barriers to conservation finance: the difficulty of proving impact. By providing reliable systems for monitoring ecosystem health, technology created the conditions for linking financial instruments to ecological performance with greater confidence. This capacity to verify outcomes in real time gave investors greater assurance that nature bonds could deliver on their promises.

The conceptual evolution of nature bonds was further informed by the rise of nature-based solutions (NBS) as a central theme in sustainability discourse. NBS emphasize the role of ecosystems in addressing climate, water, and biodiversity challenges while delivering co-benefits for communities. As NBS gained prominence in international policy and scientific discussions, it became clear that innovative financing would be required to scale them effectively. Nature bonds emerged as a tool well-suited to this purpose, explicitly linking financial flows to the maintenance and enhancement of ecosystem services that underpin resilience and adaptation.

It is important to recognize that the conceptual development of nature bonds has been iterative, shaped by dialogue among policymakers, financial institutions, conservation organizations, and communities. Early pilot projects, frameworks, and academic debates contributed to refining the definitions and scope of these instruments. Over time, consensus began to emerge around the core principles that distinguish nature bonds: measurability of outcomes, transparency in governance, and alignment with global sustainability frameworks. This collective process has ensured that the concept of nature bonds continues to evolve in response to lessons learned and emerging challenges.

In summary, the origins and conceptual development of nature bonds are rooted in the convergence of several forces: the recognition of natural capital as an asset, the precedent set by green bonds and debt-for-nature swaps, the influence of international policy frameworks, the rise of ESG investing, technological advances in monitoring, and the global emphasis on nature-based solutions. Together, these elements have given rise to a financial instrument uniquely positioned to align capital markets with ecological priorities. By embedding biodiversity and ecosystem restoration into the structure of debt instruments, nature bonds represent both a continuation of sustainable finance innovation and a step forward in integrating nature into the logic of financial systems.

Nature Bonds in the Context of Sustainable Finance

The emergence of nature bonds must be understood within the broader trajectory of sustainable finance, which seeks to align financial systems with the imperatives of environmental protection, climate action, and social equity. Sustainable finance encompasses a diverse set of instruments and strategies, from socially responsible investing to green bonds, transition finance, and blended capital mechanisms. Its unifying principle is the recognition that environmental and social factors are not externalities but integral to financial stability and long-term value creation. Within this evolving framework, nature bonds have taken shape as an instrument that places ecosystems and biodiversity at the center of investment logic.

Sustainable finance began to gain global traction in the early 2000s, accelerated by the growth of ESG investing. Institutional investors, pension funds, and sovereign wealth funds increasingly demanded vehicles that could integrate ESG criteria into traditional risk-return assessments. Green bonds became a pivotal innovation in this space, demonstrating that debt markets could be structured to support projects with clear environmental outcomes. As the green bond market expanded, however, its thematic focus often gravitated toward sectors such as energy, transport, and infrastructure. While these sectors are crucial for decarbonization, they left ecosystems and biodiversity underrepresented. This gap created the conceptual space for nature bonds, which extend sustainable finance into the realm of natural capital protection.

Nature bonds differ from other instruments within sustainable finance in their explicit connection to ecosystem services. While climate bonds may emphasize carbon emissions reduction, and sustainability-linked loans may reward general ESG performance, nature bonds tie financing directly to measurable ecological outcomes such as forest cover, watershed integrity, or habitat restoration. This distinction matters because it reorients capital flows toward areas historically marginalized in mainstream finance. By explicitly valuing biodiversity and ecosystem health, nature bonds help correct structural imbalances in sustainable finance where certain environmental goals have overshadowed others.

The integration of nature bonds into sustainable finance also reflects the growing recognition of systemic risks tied to environmental degradation. Financial institutions, regulators, and central banks have increasingly acknowledged that the loss of biodiversity and ecosystem services poses material risks to the stability of economies and financial systems. The Taskforce on Nature-related Financial Disclosures (TNFD) is a critical development in this regard, creating a framework for assessing and reporting on nature-related risks. By linking debt instruments to ecological outcomes, nature bonds align with this evolving risk management paradigm, offering investors tools to mitigate exposure to environmental instability.

In addition to risk management, nature bonds contribute to the diversification of sustainable finance portfolios. Investors are increasingly seeking products that provide not only environmental credibility but also differentiation. With green bond markets becoming highly liquid and competitive, new categories such as blue bonds, social bonds, and nature bonds offer opportunities for investors to diversify while aligning with specific impact objectives. This diversification supports the scaling of sustainable finance as a whole, expanding its scope and attracting new pools of capital.

Nature bonds also intersect with blended finance strategies, which combine public, private, and philanthropic capital to de-risk investments in sustainability. Public or multilateral entities can play a catalytic role by providing guarantees, concessional financing, or credit enhancements that make nature bonds more attractive to private investors. This blending of resources helps overcome barriers related to perceived risk and illiquidity in conservation finance. By positioning nature bonds within blended structures, sustainable finance ecosystems can mobilize larger volumes of capital toward projects that might otherwise struggle to attract investment.

Another dimension that situates nature bonds within sustainable finance is their alignment with global policy frameworks. The United Nations Sustainable Development Goals (SDGs) provide an overarching blueprint for directing capital toward sustainability objectives, and nature bonds are directly relevant to goals related to climate action, life below water, and life on land. The Paris Agreement and the Kunming-Montreal Global Biodiversity Framework further underscore the necessity of mobilizing private finance for ecological outcomes. Nature bonds operationalize these frameworks in the financial domain, creating tangible mechanisms to convert global commitments into measurable investments.

The development of taxonomies and standards within sustainable finance has also shaped the integration of nature bonds. Efforts such as the EU Taxonomy for Sustainable Activities aim to provide clarity and prevent greenwashing by defining what qualifies as environmentally sustainable. For nature bonds to succeed within this environment, they must adhere to rigorous standards that clearly demonstrate ecological impact. This requirement situates them within a broader movement in sustainable finance toward transparency, accountability, and harmonization of metrics. The credibility of nature bonds depends on their ability to meet these standards and align with evolving regulatory frameworks.

Technology plays an enabling role in connecting nature bonds to sustainable finance. Digital platforms, blockchain applications, and satellite monitoring enhance transparency and facilitate real-time verification of ecological outcomes. These innovations resonate with broader trends in sustainable finance, where data-driven tools are increasingly deployed to improve trust and accountability. The integration of advanced monitoring systems into nature bond structures ensures that they can deliver credible and verifiable results, thereby reinforcing their legitimacy within sustainable finance.

Market growth in sustainable finance has created momentum for scaling innovative products like nature bonds. Trillions of dollars have already been mobilized through green and social bonds, signaling investor appetite for sustainability-linked products. As markets mature, demand is shifting toward products with greater specificity and ecological relevance. Nature bonds respond to this evolution by offering investors opportunities to directly support biodiversity and natural capital, complementing broader sustainability goals while filling a critical niche within the financial ecosystem.

Distinction Between Nature Bonds and Other Green Instruments

Nature bonds are often compared with existing instruments in the sustainable finance landscape, particularly green bonds, blue bonds, and sustainability-linked bonds. While these instruments share the overarching goal of directing capital toward projects with environmental or social value, they differ in terms of design, scope, verification mechanisms, and the types of outcomes they prioritize. Understanding these distinctions is essential for appreciating the specific role that nature bonds play in global sustainable finance and for avoiding conceptual overlap that could dilute their unique value.

Green bonds are the closest point of comparison for nature bonds, given that they pioneered the idea of linking debt instruments with environmental outcomes. Green bonds raise capital for projects that deliver environmental benefits, most commonly renewable energy, energy efficiency, sustainable transport, and climate-resilient infrastructure. Their focus has been on reducing greenhouse gas emissions and supporting low-carbon transitions. In contrast, nature bonds target the conservation and restoration of ecosystems, biodiversity, and natural capital. Rather than focusing primarily on decarbonization, they emphasize ecological resilience, habitat preservation, and the maintenance of ecosystem services such as water filtration, carbon sequestration, and pollination. This thematic distinction situates nature bonds as complementary to green bonds rather than substitutes, broadening the environmental scope of sustainable finance.

14

Another key difference lies in the measurability of outcomes. Green bonds typically require issuers to report on outputs such as megawatts of renewable energy generated or tons of emissions avoided. These metrics, while valuable, often focus on project-level performance. Nature bonds, by contrast, necessitate ecological indicators that capture the health of ecosystems and biodiversity. Metrics might include the extent of restored forest cover, the integrity of wetlands, or the stability of species populations. Measuring these outcomes requires scientific expertise, complex monitoring systems, and long-term verification, distinguishing nature bonds from other instruments in terms of the rigor and specificity of their reporting frameworks.

Blue bonds represent another relevant category, as they are designed to support ocean-related projects such as sustainable fisheries, marine conservation, or wastewater treatment. Thematically, blue bonds share similarities with nature bonds because both focus on natural systems rather than purely technological solutions. However, blue bonds are narrower in scope, concentrating exclusively on marine and aquatic ecosystems. Nature bonds, on the other hand, encompass terrestrial, freshwater, and marine ecosystems, offering a more holistic approach to financing biodiversity and natural capital. This breadth allows nature bonds to integrate cross-ecosystem strategies, whereas blue bonds remain constrained by their ocean-centric mandate.

Sustainability-linked bonds (SLBs) provide yet another point of contrast. SLBs are not tied to specific projects but instead link the cost of financing to the issuer's achievement of predefined sustainability targets, such as reducing overall carbon emissions or improving gender diversity in leadership. Unlike green or nature bonds, which earmark proceeds for designated uses, SLBs allow issuers flexibility in how capital is deployed. Nature bonds differ in that they combine the project-specific orientation of green bonds with the outcome-based accountability of SLBs. Proceeds are earmarked for ecological projects, and repayment conditions are often tied to the achievement of measurable biodiversity or conservation outcomes. This hybrid characteristic distinguishes nature bonds as both use-of-proceeds instruments and performance-linked instruments, setting them apart from the more general frameworks of SLBs.

In terms of governance and verification, nature bonds demand higher levels of transparency than many other green instruments. While green bonds often rely on external reviewers to verify project eligibility and reporting, nature bonds require independent scientific monitoring to validate ecological outcomes. This creates a more interdisciplinary verification process, involving not only financial auditors but also ecologists, conservation scientists, and community stakeholders. The integration of ecological expertise into the governance structure reflects the complexity of the outcomes being measured and reinforces the credibility of nature bonds within the sustainable finance landscape.

The risk-return profile of nature bonds also differs from other instruments. Green bonds are typically perceived as relatively low risk, especially when issued by sovereigns or large corporations, because their outcomes are easier to measure and align closely with established financial models. Nature bonds, however, face higher levels of ecological and political risk. Ecosystem outcomes are influenced by variables such as climate variability, land-use pressures, and governance capacity, which can introduce uncertainties into performance. To address this, nature bonds often rely on credit enhancements, guarantees, or blended finance structures to make them attractive to investors. This reliance highlights their distinction from other green instruments, which may not require such complex de-risking mechanisms.

Investor motivations also highlight differences. Green bonds attract investors interested in climate mitigation, renewable energy, or general ESG compliance. Nature bonds appeal to a subset of investors seeking to directly support biodiversity, ecosystem services, and conservation outcomes. This includes mission-driven investors such as philanthropic funds, impact investors, and development finance institutions, alongside traditional institutional investors. The alignment of investor values with ecological outcomes positions nature bonds within a niche but rapidly growing segment of sustainable finance that is driven by concerns about planetary boundaries and long-term ecological resilience.

Policy frameworks further distinguish nature bonds from other instruments. Green bonds are typically aligned with climate policy frameworks such as the Paris Agreement, while nature bonds align more closely with biodiversity frameworks like the Kunming-Montreal Global Biodiversity Framework. While both sets of instruments contribute to the United Nations Sustainable Development Goals, they map onto different goals with varying degrees of emphasis. This differentiation underscores the complementary nature of these instruments, each addressing distinct aspects of the sustainability agenda.

Nature bonds also diverge in their implications for local communities. Green bonds often finance infrastructure projects with broad societal benefits, but their connection to local livelihoods may be indirect. Nature bonds, by focusing on ecosystems, intersect more directly with communities dependent on natural resources for subsistence, cultural identity, and economic opportunity. This connection requires issuers to incorporate social safeguards, participatory governance, and benefit-sharing mechanisms to ensure that financing does not create or exacerbate inequalities. The social dimension is therefore more deeply embedded in nature bonds compared to many other green instruments.

Finally, the maturity of markets differentiates these instruments. Green bonds have developed into a multi-trillion-dollar market with established taxonomies, standards, and benchmarks. Blue bonds and SLBs are newer but gaining traction with increasing issuance. Nature bonds remain at an earlier stage of development, with fewer issuances and evolving standards. Their relative novelty means they face challenges in scaling, but it also presents opportunities for innovation in structuring, verification, and integration into global financial markets. This developmental stage sets them apart from more established instruments, underscoring their potential for growth as sustainable finance continues to evolve.

Chapter 2: Financial Structures and Mechanisms

Nature bonds rely on innovative financial structures and mechanisms that integrate ecological outcomes into debt markets. Their distinctiveness lies in how they connect capital flows to biodiversity protection, ecosystem restoration, and climate resilience, using carefully designed repayment terms and performance-linked features. This chapter explores the spectrum of financial models that underpin nature bonds, from outcome-based repayment mechanisms to risk-sharing arrangements and credit enhancements. It also examines how these mechanisms attract investors by balancing ecological performance with financial returns, creating a framework in which conservation and restoration can be financed at scale while maintaining transparency and accountability.

Bond Types and Their Characteristics

Nature bonds encompass a range of structures that reflect both the innovation of sustainable finance and the unique challenges of financing biodiversity and ecosystem services. While the overarching purpose of nature bonds is to mobilize capital for conservation, restoration, and nature-based solutions, the specific type of bond issued can vary significantly depending on the issuer, the target outcomes, and the needs of investors. Understanding the diversity of bond types and their characteristics helps clarify how these instruments operate within the broader landscape of sustainability-linked finance.

One of the most prominent categories is the sovereign nature bond. These bonds are issued by national governments to finance large-scale conservation and restoration projects. Sovereign issuance is particularly important because it allows countries to mobilize significant capital while signaling a commitment to environmental stewardship. Sovereign nature bonds often align with national climate commitments, biodiversity targets, and sustainable development strategies. Their scale makes them attractive to institutional investors, while their backing by governments enhances perceived security. However, sovereign nature bonds also carry political risk, as their effectiveness depends on national governance structures, regulatory frameworks, and the consistency of policy commitments over time.

A closely related category is the sub-sovereign or municipal nature bond. These bonds are issued by local governments, regions, or cities to fund ecosystem-focused projects at a smaller geographic scale. Examples include financing for wetland restoration, watershed protection, or urban green infrastructure. Sub-sovereign bonds tend to be more localized, with impacts that directly benefit communities in the issuing jurisdiction. Their strength lies in proximity to project implementation and potential for strong community engagement. Yet, their smaller size and sometimes weaker credit profiles may limit their attractiveness to large institutional investors unless supported by guarantees or pooled structures.

Corporate nature bonds represent another important type. These are issued by private sector firms seeking to finance projects that reduce their environmental footprint or invest in ecosystem restoration as part of corporate sustainability strategies. For instance, companies in sectors such as forestry, agriculture, or natural resource management may issue nature bonds to fund sustainable land management or biodiversity offset initiatives. Corporate issuances highlight how businesses can integrate ecological stewardship into their financial operations. Their success often depends on the credibility of the issuer's sustainability commitments and the rigor of third-party verification. Corporate nature bonds may also serve as tools for companies to demonstrate alignment with ESG criteria, enhancing their brand value and access to sustainability-focused investors.

Development finance institutions (DFIs) and multilateral development banks (MDBs) have also played a catalytic role in issuing or supporting nature bonds. Bonds backed by these institutions often blend concessional finance with private capital, reducing risk for investors while ensuring high-impact projects receive funding. The participation of DFIs and MDBs enhances credibility, as these organizations are often seen as trusted intermediaries with expertise in both finance and development. Bonds linked to MDBs may incorporate features such as partial guarantees, first-loss tranches, or technical assistance facilities, which make them more attractive to private investors while advancing conservation goals in emerging markets.

Another emerging type is the thematic nature bond. These are designed around specific ecological themes such as forest bonds, wetland bonds, or biodiversity bonds. Forest bonds, for example, focus on financing reforestation, afforestation, or sustainable forest management. By targeting a single ecosystem type, thematic bonds allow issuers to appeal to investors with a strong interest in particular environmental outcomes. They also provide clarity of purpose, which can enhance transparency and reporting. However, their narrow focus may limit scalability or diversification, and they may require careful design to ensure ecological outcomes are additional and verifiable.

Performance-linked nature bonds introduce another layer of innovation. Unlike traditional use-of-proceeds bonds, these instruments tie repayment terms or interest rates to the achievement of specific ecological performance metrics. For example, a bond may stipulate that if a target for increasing forest cover or improving water quality is met, the issuer benefits from reduced repayment costs or lower coupon rates. This mechanism creates strong incentives for issuers to deliver measurable outcomes while giving investors assurance that their capital is tied to real ecological impact. The performance-linked design aligns closely with the broader trend of sustainability-linked bonds but retains a sharper focus on ecosystems and biodiversity.

Hybrid structures are increasingly common in the design of nature bonds. These combine features of multiple categories, such as use-of-proceeds commitments with performance-linked conditions. A hybrid nature bond might earmark capital for a reforestation project while also linking coupon adjustments to biodiversity indicators. This dual structure enhances both accountability and flexibility, offering investors confidence in the use of funds while incentivizing issuers to achieve measurable outcomes. Hybrids are particularly well suited to projects with both high upfront capital needs and long-term ecological performance goals.

Credit-enhanced nature bonds form another subset, designed to mitigate the risks associated with ecological projects. Because ecosystem outcomes can be uncertain and influenced by external factors such as climate variability or political instability, credit enhancements play a key role in attracting investors. Enhancements may include guarantees from MDBs, first-loss tranches from philanthropic organizations, or insurance mechanisms that protect investors against default. These structures make nature bonds more competitive in financial markets and broaden the pool of potential investors beyond those exclusively focused on impact.

Community-based nature bonds highlight the potential of scaling down financial structures to engage local stakeholders directly. These smaller-scale issuances may be designed to finance conservation initiatives managed by cooperatives, community groups, or indigenous organizations. While their size limits their appeal to large institutional investors, community-based bonds can attract retail investors, philanthropic organizations, or specialized impact funds. Their strength lies in fostering local ownership, ensuring that conservation benefits directly reach those who depend most on ecosystems. The challenge, however, lies in structuring these bonds with sufficient governance and verification systems to satisfy investor requirements while keeping transaction costs manageable.

Finally, digital or tokenized nature bonds are beginning to emerge, reflecting broader trends in financial innovation. Tokenization allows bonds to be issued and traded on digital platforms, potentially expanding access to smaller investors while increasing liquidity. Blockchain technology can also enhance transparency by embedding performance metrics and monitoring data directly into bond structures. While still experimental, digital bonds have the potential to reduce transaction costs, democratize access, and integrate real-time ecological monitoring into financial instruments.

The diversity of bond types underscores the flexibility of nature bonds as tools for financing conservation and climate action. From sovereign and corporate issuances to thematic and digital structures, each type carries distinct advantages and challenges. This diversity allows issuers and investors to tailor nature bond designs to specific contexts, risk profiles, and ecological priorities, making them adaptable instruments within the expanding field of sustainable finance.

Risk-Sharing and Credit Enhancements

Risk-sharing and credit enhancement mechanisms are central to the design and scaling of nature bonds. Ecosystem conservation and biodiversity restoration are complex activities that face uncertainties related to ecological performance, political stability, and long-term financial sustainability. These risks can deter private investors who are accustomed to more predictable asset classes. To overcome these barriers, issuers and intermediaries employ a range of risk-sharing arrangements and credit enhancement tools that improve the attractiveness of nature bonds while safeguarding their integrity.

Risk-sharing in the context of nature bonds involves distributing potential losses or uncertainties among multiple stakeholders. Governments, MDBs, philanthropic organizations, and private investors often collaborate to structure financing that balances risk and reward. Public entities may accept a greater share of the risk in order to mobilize private capital at scale. For example, sovereign or sub-sovereign issuers can provide guarantees or backstops, ensuring repayment even if ecological outcomes are not fully realized. By absorbing a portion of the downside risk, public institutions create conditions that encourage private investors to participate in financing conservation projects that might otherwise appear too risky.

Credit enhancements are specific mechanisms designed to improve the creditworthiness of a bond. They reassure investors that they will be repaid and that the issuer is capable of meeting obligations, even under uncertain ecological or political conditions. One common form of credit enhancement is a partial guarantee provided by an MDB or DFI. Such guarantees can cover a portion of the principal or interest payments in the event of default. This reduces the perceived credit risk of the bond, making it more attractive to a wider pool of investors, including those with more conservative mandates.

First-loss capital structures are another important credit enhancement tool. In this arrangement, a portion of the financing—often provided by philanthropic foundations or concessional finance from public institutions—is designated to absorb initial losses. This layer of capital effectively protects senior investors by ensuring that their exposure is limited. The presence of first-loss capital lowers the risk profile of the bond and makes it easier to raise larger volumes of private capital. This layered approach to risk-sharing has been particularly effective in blended finance, where diverse capital sources are combined to maximize impact.

Insurance mechanisms also play a role in credit enhancement for nature bonds. Insurance products can cover risks such as natural disasters, political instability, or default by the issuer. For example, parametric insurance can provide payouts when specific environmental or climatic conditions occur, reducing the financial impact of unpredictable events on conservation projects. By transferring certain risks to insurance markets, issuers of nature bonds can provide greater certainty to investors, thereby lowering required yields and improving market access.

Escrow accounts and reserve funds represent additional credit enhancement features. Issuers can establish accounts where a portion of proceeds or revenues are set aside as security for repayment. This provides investors with confidence that funds are available even if project revenues fall short. Reserve funds are particularly valuable for projects with long timelines, such as forest restoration, where ecological and financial returns may take decades to materialize. By pre-funding repayment commitments, issuers mitigate concerns about long-term uncertainty.

The role of MDBs and DFIs in providing credit enhancements cannot be overstated. These institutions often act as anchors in bond issuances, lending credibility and signaling that the instrument aligns with global sustainability goals. Their participation not only reduces risk but also attracts other investors by demonstrating international support and oversight. MDBs can also offer technical assistance to strengthen project design, monitoring, and reporting, thereby improving the likelihood of achieving ecological outcomes and ensuring compliance with bond terms.

Risk-sharing arrangements also extend to governance structures. In many nature bond designs, responsibilities for monitoring and verification are distributed among independent parties, reducing the potential for conflicts of interest. By sharing responsibility for oversight, issuers enhance transparency and accountability, which in turn reduces reputational risks for investors. Independent verification of ecological outcomes ensures that repayments or coupon adjustments linked to performance are based on credible evidence, reinforcing investor confidence.

Investor diversification is another dimension of risk-sharing. By attracting a mix of institutional investors, impact funds, and philanthropic organizations, issuers can spread risk across different types of capital providers. Some investors may prioritize financial returns, while others are more focused on impact, allowing for structures that balance these objectives. Retail investors can also participate through pooled vehicles or digital platforms, further broadening the investor base and distributing exposure across a larger group.

Credit enhancements and risk-sharing mechanisms must be carefully designed to avoid moral hazard, where issuers rely too heavily on guarantees or subsidies without maintaining strong incentives to achieve ecological outcomes. Effective structures ensure that issuers remain accountable for delivering on environmental commitments while providing sufficient protections to reassure investors. This balance is critical to maintaining both credibility and scalability in the market for nature bonds.

The use of risk-sharing and credit enhancements also reflects a broader trend in sustainable finance toward blended approaches. Conservation projects often face a mismatch between the high upfront costs of implementation and the delayed realization of ecological and financial benefits. Blended finance solutions, supported by public and philanthropic actors, bridge this gap by absorbing early-stage risks and creating space for private capital to engage. Nature bonds, with their reliance on ecological performance, are particularly suited to such structures, as they inherently involve long-term horizons and complex variables.

Overall, risk-sharing and credit enhancements are indispensable to the success of nature bonds. They provide the tools to mitigate ecological, political, and financial risks while ensuring that projects remain attractive to diverse investors. By combining guarantees, first-loss capital, insurance, reserves, and blended finance strategies, issuers can design instruments that are both credible and scalable. These mechanisms make it possible to channel significant volumes of capital into biodiversity and ecosystem restoration, addressing funding gaps that traditional finance has been unable to fill.

Linking Repayment to Environmental Outcomes

A defining feature of nature bonds is their linkage between financial repayment and environmental outcomes. Unlike conventional debt instruments, which rely solely on the issuer's ability to generate revenue or fiscal capacity, nature bonds embed ecological performance into their repayment structures. This innovation creates a powerful alignment between financial markets and environmental stewardship, as the issuer's financial obligations are directly influenced by measurable conservation or restoration results. Such linkages enhance accountability, increase transparency, and ensure that nature bonds contribute tangible value to ecosystems and biodiversity.

At the core of this design is the principle of conditionality. Traditional use-of-proceeds bonds specify how funds must be allocated but do not necessarily tie repayment terms to outcomes. In contrast, nature bonds often link coupon rates, repayment schedules, or principal reductions to the achievement of ecological targets. For example, if a government or corporation issuing a bond meets predefined milestones—such as restoring a specified number of hectares of forest or improving water quality in a watershed—then the financial cost of the bond may be reduced. This mechanism creates direct financial incentives for issuers to achieve environmental results while rewarding investors with impact assurance.

The measurement of outcomes is central to this process. Linking repayment to environmental performance requires robust metrics that are both scientifically valid and practically measurable. Common indicators include forest cover, carbon sequestration levels, biodiversity indices, or water quality measures. These metrics must be carefully selected to balance precision with feasibility. Too narrow a metric may overlook broader ecosystem benefits, while too broad a measure may prove difficult to monitor and verify. The choice of metrics is therefore a critical step in structuring nature bonds, requiring collaboration between ecologists, financial experts, and policymakers.

Verification mechanisms provide credibility to outcome-linked repayment structures. Independent third-party organizations often conduct monitoring and verification to ensure that reported outcomes are accurate and free from manipulation. Advances in technology, such as satellite imagery, drones, and remote sensing, have made it easier to track ecological changes over time. These tools provide objective data that can be integrated into bond contracts, creating a direct link between environmental performance and financial terms. Independent verification not only reassures investors but also strengthens the legitimacy of the instrument within the broader sustainable finance ecosystem.

Repayment structures can take multiple forms depending on the design of the bond. One model is the step-down coupon, where the interest rate decreases if ecological targets are achieved. This provides issuers with a financial reward for meeting environmental goals. Another model involves partial principal forgiveness, where a portion of the bond's value is reduced if specific outcomes are delivered. This approach can be particularly attractive in sovereign contexts, where governments face high debt burdens. A third model links repayment schedules to performance, allowing issuers more time to repay if environmental milestones are reached. Each of these structures incentivizes ecological performance while providing flexibility to align with the issuer's financial capacity.

Risk-sharing plays a critical role in linking repayment to outcomes. Conservation and restoration projects are inherently subject to external variables such as climate variability, political instability, and market fluctuations. To address this, many nature bond designs incorporate blended finance structures where public or philanthropic capital absorbs some of the risks associated with outcome uncertainty. For example, first-loss guarantees can protect investors in cases where ecological targets are partially unmet due to unforeseen circumstances. This arrangement ensures that repayment structures remain credible while acknowledging the inherent uncertainty of environmental systems.

The integration of repayment conditionality with global policy frameworks enhances the relevance of nature bonds. Linking repayment to outcomes aligned with the Paris Agreement or the Kunming-Montreal Global Biodiversity Framework creates a clear connection between national commitments and financial instruments. Governments can demonstrate progress toward international targets while simultaneously improving their credit terms. For investors, this alignment provides assurance that their capital is contributing to globally recognized goals, increasing the legitimacy and attractiveness of nature bonds as part of sustainable portfolios.

Social dimensions also influence the design of outcome-linked repayment structures. Many conservation and restoration projects affect local communities, particularly indigenous peoples and those directly dependent on ecosystems. To ensure equitable benefits, repayment structures can incorporate social performance indicators alongside ecological ones. For instance, a bond might reward issuers not only for restoring forest cover but also for securing land tenure rights for indigenous communities or improving livelihoods through sustainable resource management. Integrating social outcomes strengthens the legitimacy of the bond and enhances its long-term sustainability by ensuring local support.

Linking repayment to outcomes also addresses concerns about greenwashing, a persistent challenge in sustainable finance. By conditioning financial benefits on verified results, nature bonds reduce the risk that issuers will overstate or misrepresent environmental impacts. The direct financial consequences of failing to achieve ecological targets act as a safeguard against superficial commitments. Investors gain greater confidence that their capital is contributing to real and measurable impact, distinguishing nature bonds from less rigorous instruments in the green finance space.

Flexibility in repayment structures is another important characteristic. Ecosystems evolve over long time horizons, and ecological outcomes may take years or even decades to materialize. To accommodate this, nature bonds can include adaptive mechanisms that adjust repayment terms based on interim milestones or rolling assessments. For example, partial coupon reductions may be triggered by incremental progress toward reforestation goals, rather than requiring full completion before benefits are realized. This phased approach provides issuers with ongoing incentives while offering investors a steady flow of verified impact.

The success of outcome-linked repayment also depends on strong governance frameworks. Transparent reporting, stakeholder engagement, and legal enforceability are essential to ensuring that repayment terms are respected. Governance structures often involve multi-stakeholder committees that oversee monitoring and verification processes, integrating input from governments, investors, scientific institutions, and local communities. These arrangements reinforce accountability and prevent disputes over whether targets have been met, further strengthening the credibility of the instrument.

Financial innovation continues to expand the possibilities for linking repayment to outcomes. Tokenized or digital nature bonds can embed repayment conditions directly into smart contracts, automatically adjusting coupon payments based on verified data from remote sensing or monitoring platforms. Such innovations enhance efficiency, reduce transaction costs, and ensure timely alignment between ecological performance and financial terms. As technology evolves, these digital mechanisms may become a standard feature of outcome-linked repayment systems.

Overall, linking repayment to environmental outcomes differentiates nature bonds from other instruments in sustainable finance. By embedding ecological performance directly into financial structures, these bonds transform conservation into a core component of creditworthiness and financial planning. For issuers, outcome-linked repayment provides incentives to deliver measurable impact. For investors, it ensures accountability and transparency, reducing reputational and impact risks. By tying financial obligations to the health of ecosystems, nature bonds align the interests of financial markets with the imperatives of ecological stewardship, reshaping how capital flows are directed toward sustainability.

Chapter 3: Governance, Oversight, and Risk Management

Governance and oversight mechanisms are central to the credibility and long-term viability of nature bonds. Investors require assurance that funds are used appropriately, ecological outcomes are accurately measured, and social safeguards are respected. This chapter examines the frameworks that underpin effective governance in nature bond markets, highlighting the role of independent verification, regulatory authorities, and risk-sharing arrangements. It explores how accountability structures protect against greenwashing, how oversight enhances transparency, and how risk management tools balance ecological uncertainty with financial stability. Together, these mechanisms create the trust and legitimacy needed to scale nature bonds globally.

Role of Governments and Regulatory Authorities

Governments and regulatory authorities play a pivotal role in shaping the development, credibility, and scalability of nature bonds. As custodians of public policy and financial oversight, they provide the enabling frameworks that allow these instruments to function within national and international financial systems. Their involvement is not limited to issuing bonds; it also extends to setting standards, establishing legal frameworks, providing incentives, and ensuring that environmental and financial objectives are aligned. Without strong governmental and regulatory participation, the ability of nature bonds to attract significant capital and deliver ecological outcomes would remain constrained.

A fundamental responsibility of governments in the context of nature bonds is to establish the policy and legal frameworks that define their legitimacy. Conservation and biodiversity financing require clear laws that safeguard ecosystems and assign responsibility for their protection. Governments can strengthen investor confidence by enacting legislation that ensures proceeds from nature bonds are used transparently and exclusively for conservation or restoration projects. Legal frameworks that protect land tenure, clarify property rights, and secure indigenous and community rights also provide essential safeguards, reducing the risk of disputes that could undermine the financial and ecological performance of nature bonds.

Regulatory authorities are tasked with integrating nature bonds into broader financial markets. Securities regulators, central banks, and financial supervisory bodies must create mechanisms that allow nature bonds to be listed, traded, and monitored with the same rigor as other debt instruments. This includes defining disclosure requirements, establishing standardized reporting formats, and ensuring compliance with international norms for sustainable finance. Regulators can also prevent the misuse of nature bond labels by enforcing strict criteria that distinguish genuine conservation-linked instruments from those that merely claim environmental benefits without substantiating them. By setting clear standards, regulators reduce the risk of greenwashing and reinforce the credibility of the market.

Governments also serve as issuers of nature bonds, particularly in the sovereign context. Sovereign issuance signals national commitment to biodiversity protection and mobilizes significant capital for large-scale conservation initiatives. In doing so, governments can align bond proceeds with national biodiversity strategies, nationally determined contributions (NDCs) under the Paris Agreement, and the Sustainable Development Goals. The sovereign role is especially important in emerging markets, where access to private capital may be limited and government leadership can act as a catalyst for broader investment. By issuing sovereign nature bonds, governments demonstrate accountability both to their citizens and to the international community.

Another critical function of governments and regulatory authorities is the provision of financial incentives that enhance the attractiveness of nature bonds. Tax exemptions, subsidies, or preferential treatment for investors can stimulate demand and expand the investor base. Central banks may also play a role by including nature bonds in their asset purchase programs or recognizing them as eligible collateral, thereby signaling their legitimacy within monetary policy frameworks. Development agencies and ministries of finance can provide credit enhancements, guarantees, or co-financing that reduce risk and improve credit ratings, making nature bonds accessible to a wider range of investors.

Monitoring and verification are additional areas where governments and regulators exert influence. Ensuring that ecological outcomes are measurable, verifiable, and reported transparently requires institutions capable of overseeing monitoring systems and enforcing accountability. Regulatory authorities can establish guidelines for independent verification, mandate the use of credible third-party assessors, and require periodic disclosure of progress toward ecological targets. In many jurisdictions, environmental agencies may collaborate with financial regulators to ensure that monitoring systems integrate scientific rigor with financial reporting requirements. This intersection of environmental and financial governance is essential to the integrity of nature bonds.

Governments also shape the global policy environment in which nature bonds operate. Through participation in international agreements, they commit to frameworks that provide a rationale and structure for biodiversity finance. Agreements such as the Kunming-Montreal Global Biodiversity Framework and the Paris Agreement create demand for innovative financing mechanisms, including nature bonds. Governments can incorporate nature bonds into national financing strategies to meet these commitments, thereby reinforcing international cooperation while mobilizing domestic resources. Regulatory authorities, by harmonizing national regulations with global taxonomies and disclosure standards, ensure that nature bonds issued within their jurisdictions are compatible with international markets.

Capacity building represents another dimension of governmental responsibility. Many countries, particularly in the Global South, lack the technical expertise and institutional infrastructure to design, issue, and monitor nature bonds. Governments can address this by investing in training, establishing specialized agencies or units, and collaborating with multilateral development banks and international organizations. Regulatory authorities can also foster knowledge-sharing platforms that disseminate best practices and lessons learned across jurisdictions. By strengthening institutional capacity, governments enable a broader range of actors to participate in the market for nature bonds.

Governments further contribute by fostering public-private partnerships that bring together diverse stakeholders in the issuance and management of nature bonds. Ministries of finance, environmental agencies, and regulators can collaborate with corporations, banks, and civil society organizations to co-design instruments that balance financial viability with ecological integrity. Public-private partnerships are particularly valuable in contexts where conservation projects intersect with local communities. Governments can ensure that these partnerships incorporate social safeguards, benefit-sharing mechanisms, and participatory governance structures that enhance legitimacy and long-term sustainability.

Finally, governments and regulatory authorities serve a signaling function that extends beyond the technical aspects of issuance and oversight. Their active involvement sends a strong message to markets that nature bonds are credible, legitimate, and aligned with national and global priorities. This signaling effect is crucial for building investor confidence and expanding the market. When governments demonstrate commitment through regulatory clarity, fiscal incentives, sovereign issuance, and rigorous oversight, they create the conditions for scaling nature bonds from niche instruments into mainstream components of sustainable finance.

Independent Verification and Monitoring Systems

Independent verification and monitoring systems form the backbone of credibility in the issuance and operation of nature bonds. Investors and stakeholders require confidence that the ecological outcomes promised in bond structures are not only pursued but achieved with measurable integrity. Without rigorous oversight, the risk of greenwashing increases, undermining both investor trust and the effectiveness of conservation financing. Independent verification therefore ensures that repayment structures, reporting, and environmental outcomes remain transparent and accountable across the life of the instrument.

At the center of these systems is the principle of third-party oversight. Independent verification separates issuers from evaluators, minimizing conflicts of interest and ensuring that reported progress is reliable. Specialized organizations, including environmental consultancies, auditing firms, and accredited certification bodies, are often tasked with monitoring ecological indicators tied to nature bonds. Their independence provides assurance that the environmental performance claims made by issuers are valid, thereby protecting investor confidence and maintaining the legitimacy of the market.

Monitoring systems are designed to capture ecological outcomes in ways that can be quantified, compared, and tracked over time. Indicators typically include measures of forest cover, biodiversity levels, water quality, soil health, or carbon sequestration. The design of these indicators must balance scientific accuracy with practical feasibility. To meet this need, independent monitoring bodies often work closely with ecologists and conservation scientists to develop metrics that reflect both ecological integrity and investor requirements for measurability. This collaboration ensures that indicators are robust, transparent, and resistant to manipulation.

Technology plays an increasingly important role in verification systems. Remote sensing through satellites, drones, and geographic information systems (GIS) allows independent verifiers to monitor large and remote ecosystems at scale. These tools provide real-time or near-real-time data on land use, vegetation cover, and ecosystem changes. Such data can be cross-referenced with ground-based surveys conducted by independent ecological teams, ensuring accuracy and accountability. Advances in digital platforms and blockchain further enhance transparency by enabling investors to directly access monitoring data, creating immutable records of ecological performance that are resistant to tampering.

Periodic reporting is a critical component of independent monitoring systems. Issuers of nature bonds are typically required to provide regular updates on ecological progress, which are then subject to independent review. These reports may be annual or biannual and include detailed assessments of whether ecological targets are being met. Independent verification bodies review these reports, confirm their accuracy, and publish findings in ways that are accessible to investors. By institutionalizing cycles of reporting and review, monitoring systems maintain ongoing accountability rather than limiting oversight to the bond's issuance phase.

Another dimension of independent verification involves compliance with established international standards. Frameworks such as the International Capital Market Association (ICMA) Green Bond Principles and the Climate Bonds Standard provide guidance on structuring sustainable finance instruments. Nature bonds often align with these frameworks but extend them by incorporating biodiversity-specific indicators. Independent certification against these standards ensures that nature bonds meet recognized best practices and reduces the risk of reputational damage for both issuers and investors.

Governance structures often include multi-stakeholder committees that oversee monitoring and verification. These committees may include representatives from governments, financial institutions, conservation organizations, and local communities. By diversifying participation, governance bodies enhance legitimacy and reduce the concentration of power. Independent verifiers report to these committees, ensuring that findings are reviewed transparently and acted upon where necessary. The multi-stakeholder model also strengthens social accountability, particularly when projects affect local communities or indigenous groups.

Challenges remain in implementing independent verification systems effectively. Ecosystem outcomes often take years or decades to materialize, creating difficulties for short-term monitoring cycles. External factors such as climate variability, natural disasters, or political changes can also affect outcomes, complicating assessments of issuer performance. Independent monitoring systems must therefore be designed to distinguish between failures of governance and natural variability, ensuring fairness in outcome-linked repayment structures. Addressing these challenges requires adaptive monitoring approaches that evolve with ecological and financial realities.

Costs are another factor influencing verification systems. Independent monitoring and certification can be resource-intensive, particularly in remote or complex ecosystems. These costs may deter smaller issuers or limit the scalability of nature bonds in lower-income countries. To address this, blended finance models sometimes cover monitoring expenses through concessional funding or philanthropic contributions, ensuring that robust verification is not compromised by financial constraints. Efforts to streamline monitoring processes through technology and standardized reporting frameworks also reduce costs while maintaining rigor.

Independent verification and monitoring systems also play a role in building long-term investor confidence. By providing transparent, credible, and consistent data, these systems enable investors to assess the environmental performance of nature bonds alongside financial returns. Over time, such assurance helps deepen markets, attract new investors, and integrate nature bonds into mainstream investment portfolios. Monitoring systems therefore serve not only as compliance tools but as enablers of market growth, reinforcing the stability and legitimacy of nature bonds as a financing mechanism for conservation and biodiversity.

Transparency and Investor Confidence

Transparency and investor confidence are essential pillars for the success of nature bonds. Unlike traditional financial instruments, which are primarily judged on creditworthiness and repayment capacity, nature bonds rely on their ability to demonstrate verifiable ecological outcomes. This creates a heightened need for transparent reporting, credible data, and clear communication. Investors must be assured that their capital is genuinely contributing to conservation and restoration while also being safeguarded by sound financial practices. The interplay between transparency and investor confidence determines both the attractiveness of these instruments and their long-term viability in global markets.

A first dimension of transparency in nature bonds relates to the use of proceeds. Investors require clarity on how funds are allocated, ensuring that every dollar raised is directed toward the specified ecological objectives. Issuers are therefore expected to provide detailed disclosure at the time of issuance, specifying the categories of projects to be financed, the expected environmental benefits, and the governance mechanisms in place to oversee fund allocation. Ongoing disclosure throughout the life of the bond reinforces accountability, with issuers reporting regularly on how proceeds are deployed and what progress has been achieved.

Transparency also extends to the measurement of ecological outcomes. Nature bonds rely on indicators that capture the health and resilience of ecosystems, such as forest regeneration, water quality, or biodiversity levels. Investors need assurance that these indicators are chosen with scientific rigor and measured consistently over time. Clear methodologies for defining baselines, monitoring progress, and assessing impact help ensure comparability across issuances. Without transparency in methodologies, investors face uncertainty about the reliability of reported outcomes, which could undermine confidence in the market as a whole.

Third-party verification strengthens transparency by ensuring that issuer claims are independently validated. Independent auditors, scientific institutions, and specialized environmental organizations play a crucial role in confirming that ecological outcomes have been achieved. These verifiers enhance the credibility of reported results, mitigating the risk of overstated impacts or misallocated funds. For investors, the involvement of independent verifiers reduces reputational and impact risk, providing assurance that their investments deliver genuine conservation outcomes. Transparency is therefore reinforced not only by issuer disclosure but also by impartial oversight.

Regulatory frameworks further underpin transparency and confidence. Securities regulators and financial authorities require issuers to disclose relevant information, creating a legal foundation for investor protection. The development of taxonomies and reporting standards, such as those established in the European Union or through the TNFD, provides common guidelines that issuers must follow. These frameworks reduce ambiguity and ensure that investors can compare bonds across issuers and jurisdictions. Clear standards also help prevent greenwashing, which could otherwise erode confidence in the integrity of nature bonds.

Investor confidence depends not only on disclosure but also on the predictability of financial returns. Transparent information on how repayment terms are linked to ecological outcomes is critical. Investors must understand in advance how their returns will be affected if targets are met, partially achieved, or missed. This includes clarity on coupon step-downs, principal reductions, or other performance-linked features. By clearly communicating these mechanisms, issuers reduce uncertainty and build trust that financial terms are fair, transparent, and enforceable.

The accessibility of information also shapes investor perceptions. Comprehensive reporting that is publicly available and presented in a clear, standardized format strengthens transparency and widens participation. Investors from diverse backgrounds, including institutional investors, impact funds, and retail participants, can engage more confidently when data is presented consistently and without excessive complexity. Digital platforms that provide real-time access to ecological monitoring data further enhance this accessibility, allowing investors to directly observe progress.

Reputation plays a central role in investor confidence. Issuers with strong track records in sustainability and credible governance structures are more likely to attract investor trust. Conversely, lack of transparency in prior issuances or poorly designed reporting frameworks can deter participation. To build and sustain investor confidence, issuers must demonstrate not only compliance with reporting standards but also a genuine commitment to environmental stewardship. Consistency between stated objectives and demonstrated actions is critical to reinforcing credibility in the eyes of investors.

Transparency is also tied to risk management. Investors must understand not only the potential ecological benefits but also the risks that could affect bond performance. These include ecological risks such as droughts or fires, financial risks related to currency fluctuations, and political risks such as changes in governance. Transparent disclosure of risks, along with the mitigation measures in place, strengthens investor confidence by showing that issuers are proactively managing potential challenges. The absence of clear risk disclosure, by contrast, creates uncertainty and weakens trust.

Engagement with stakeholders beyond investors enhances transparency and confidence. Local communities, civil society organizations, and international agencies all have an interest in the outcomes of conservation finance. By involving these stakeholders in reporting and oversight processes, issuers reinforce accountability and build broader legitimacy. For investors, the knowledge that projects are supported and monitored by diverse stakeholders provides additional assurance that ecological and social outcomes will be delivered.

In sum, transparency contributes to the growth and maturity of the nature bond market. Early issuances set precedents for disclosure and accountability, shaping investor expectations and influencing future market standards. Consistent transparency across issuances creates comparability, which in turn enhances market liquidity and attracts larger pools of capital. As investor confidence deepens, nature bonds can transition from niche instruments to mainstream sustainable finance products, mobilizing greater volumes of capital for conservation and restoration efforts.

Chapter 4: Integrating Nature Bonds into Global Climate Action

Nature bonds have the potential to become a vital instrument within the broader framework of international climate strategies. By linking capital markets to biodiversity protection and ecosystem restoration, they directly contribute to goals of mitigation, adaptation, and resilience. This chapter explores how nature bonds align with the Paris Agreement, nationally determined contributions, and emerging biodiversity commitments, highlighting their role in bridging finance gaps. It also examines how these instruments complement existing climate finance tools, enabling governments, investors, and institutions to mobilize resources at scale while ensuring coherence with global sustainability objectives.

Alignment with the Paris Agreement

The Paris Agreement, adopted in 2015, established a global framework for addressing climate change by limiting temperature rise to well below 2°C and pursuing efforts to restrict it to 1.5°C above pre-industrial levels. Central to this framework is the recognition that financial flows must be made consistent with pathways toward low greenhouse gas emissions and climate-resilient development. Nature bonds align closely with this mandate, offering a mechanism to channel capital into ecosystem-based solutions that support both mitigation and adaptation objectives. Their role in financing conservation, restoration, and sustainable resource management directly contributes to the goals and spirit of the Paris Agreement.

A critical dimension of alignment lies in the support that nature bonds provide to NDCs. Under the Paris framework, countries submit NDCs that outline their climate commitments, which often include targets for reforestation, sustainable agriculture, or ecosystem protection. Financing these targets remains a significant challenge, particularly for developing countries with limited fiscal space. Nature bonds can serve as a practical tool for mobilizing private and public capital toward achieving NDC objectives. By structuring repayment terms around verified ecological outcomes, such as carbon sequestration or land restoration, nature bonds provide a direct link between national commitments and financial instruments.

Nature bonds also advance the adaptation agenda of the Paris Agreement. Ecosystem restoration and conservation strengthen resilience by reducing vulnerability to climate impacts such as floods, droughts, and storms. Wetlands, mangroves, and forests act as natural buffers, providing cost-effective alternatives or complements to engineered infrastructure. By financing these solutions, nature bonds help countries implement adaptation strategies that reduce long-term risks for communities and economies. Adaptation financing has historically lagged behind mitigation, and instruments like nature bonds provide an opportunity to close this gap while ensuring that ecosystems remain functional and resilient.

Mitigation benefits are equally central to the alignment between nature bonds and the Paris Agreement. Forests, soils, and other ecosystems serve as carbon sinks, sequestering large amounts of greenhouse gases. Protecting and restoring these systems is essential for achieving net-zero pathways. Nature bonds that finance afforestation, reforestation, or sustainable land use directly contribute to emission reductions and carbon storage. Unlike some mitigation projects focused solely on technological solutions, nature-based approaches deliver co-benefits for biodiversity, water, and livelihoods, reinforcing the integrated approach envisioned by the Paris Agreement.

Transparency and accountability are critical elements of the Paris framework, and nature bonds support these through their reliance on independent verification and robust monitoring systems. Countries are required to track and report progress toward their NDCs, and instruments like nature bonds provide a structured mechanism for doing so. By linking financial terms to verified outcomes, nature bonds create incentives for accurate reporting and discourage overstatement of progress. This enhances the credibility of national climate reporting while aligning domestic financing mechanisms with international transparency requirements.

The principle of equity, embedded in the Paris Agreement, also intersects with the design of nature bonds. Many developing countries face disproportionate vulnerabilities to climate change while having contributed the least to global emissions. Nature bonds provide a means of channeling international capital to these countries, often with support from multilateral development banks or blended finance arrangements that reduce risk for private investors. By facilitating investment in ecosystems that support both mitigation and adaptation, nature bonds operationalize the principle of common but differentiated responsibilities, helping balance global equity in climate action.

Regulatory and policy coherence further strengthen the alignment between nature bonds and the Paris Agreement. Governments that integrate nature bonds into national climate finance strategies demonstrate their commitment to mobilizing diverse sources of capital for achieving NDCs. Ministries of environment, finance, and planning can collaborate to design bond frameworks that reflect national climate priorities while complying with financial market regulations. This coherence enhances both the credibility of national climate strategies and the attractiveness of nature bonds to investors seeking assurance that instruments are backed by strong policy commitments.

Another area of alignment is the mobilization of long-term finance. The Paris Agreement emphasizes the importance of shifting trillions of dollars in global capital flows toward climate-compatible pathways. Traditional sources of climate finance, such as grants or concessional loans, remain insufficient to meet the scale of the challenge. Nature bonds contribute to this shift by unlocking new streams of private capital, leveraging public and philanthropic contributions, and creating scalable mechanisms for conservation finance. By embedding climate outcomes into bond repayment structures, they transform ecosystems into credible investment opportunities, advancing the financial reorientation called for by the Paris framework.

Investor demand for Paris-aligned instruments is also driving the development of nature bonds. Institutional investors increasingly seek opportunities that demonstrate clear alignment with global climate goals. Taxonomies, disclosure requirements, and portfolio alignment tools developed in the wake of the Paris Agreement encourage investors to scrutinize whether their holdings are consistent with a 1.5°C pathway. Nature bonds, by financing verifiable ecosystem-based mitigation and adaptation outcomes, provide products that satisfy these investor mandates. Their design allows investors to demonstrate alignment with international climate goals while diversifying portfolios across new asset classes.

The integration of nature bonds with global carbon markets creates another point of connection with the Paris framework. Article 6 of the Paris Agreement establishes mechanisms for international cooperation in carbon trading. Projects financed through nature bonds can generate verified carbon credits, which may be traded under these mechanisms. By linking bond financing with carbon market revenues, issuers create additional incentives for conservation and restoration while contributing to the global effort to reduce emissions cost-effectively. This integration further situates nature bonds within the financial architecture of the Paris Agreement.

Nature bonds also support the broader ambition of the Paris Agreement by fostering systemic transformation. Climate resilience and mitigation cannot be achieved solely through technological or energy-sector interventions; they require fundamental shifts in how societies value and manage ecosystems. By embedding natural capital into financial structures, nature bonds contribute to mainstreaming ecological considerations in economic decision-making. This reorientation reflects the integrated, cross-sectoral approach that the Paris Agreement encourages, where climate action is inseparable from sustainable development and biodiversity protection.

Supporting Nationally Determined Contributions

NDCs are at the heart of the Paris Agreement, serving as the primary vehicles through which countries communicate their climate action commitments. Each NDC outlines specific mitigation and adaptation targets tailored to national circumstances and priorities. While ambition levels vary, the collective goal is to place the world on a pathway consistent with limiting temperature rise and building resilience to climate impacts. Financing these commitments, however, remains a persistent challenge. Nature bonds provide a mechanism to mobilize the necessary capital by directly linking financial flows to the achievement of NDC-related outcomes.

A first dimension of support comes through mobilizing investment for mitigation activities. Many NDCs include targets for reforestation, afforestation, or sustainable land management, which are central to enhancing carbon sinks and reducing emissions. Nature bonds can be structured to finance such activities, with repayment terms tied to verifiable increases in forest cover, soil carbon storage, or ecosystem integrity. By embedding these outcomes into the financial architecture of the bond, issuers create direct accountability for achieving NDC goals while offering investors a transparent measure of impact.

Adaptation is another critical component of NDCs that aligns with nature bond financing. Countries frequently highlight the need to enhance resilience in sectors such as agriculture, water, and coastal protection. Ecosystem-based adaptation strategies—including mangrove restoration, watershed management, and agroforestry—play a central role in these plans. Nature bonds can channel capital toward these strategies, supporting the adaptation priorities laid out in NDCs. By financing ecosystems that buffer against floods, droughts, and storms, nature bonds contribute to reducing vulnerability and safeguarding livelihoods, addressing the adaptation finance gap that many countries continue to face.

The flexibility of nature bonds allows them to respond to diverse NDC contexts. In high-income countries, bonds can fund large-scale restoration or conservation programs that complement existing climate policies. In developing countries, they can provide access to capital for projects that would otherwise remain underfunded, especially when combined with credit enhancements or blended finance. This adaptability ensures that nature bonds can be tailored to national circumstances while maintaining alignment with global climate goals.

Integration with national climate finance strategies strengthens the role of nature bonds in supporting NDCs. Ministries of environment and finance can collaborate to embed nature bond frameworks into national development plans, ensuring coherence between climate commitments and financial instruments. This alignment demonstrates to investors that bonds are not isolated initiatives but part of a broader, government-backed strategy to achieve Paris Agreement targets. Such integration enhances credibility, reduces policy risk, and signals long-term commitment to sustainable finance.

Transparency and accountability are central to the credibility of NDCs, and nature bonds reinforce these principles through their outcome-linked repayment structures. Independent monitoring and verification of ecological targets provide governments with reliable data that can also feed into NDC reporting processes. This dual function—supporting both investor confidence and national reporting obligations—creates efficiencies and strengthens the quality of climate reporting. By embedding rigorous monitoring systems, nature bonds help governments demonstrate measurable progress toward their international commitments.

Nature bonds also support NDC implementation by unlocking international capital flows. Many developing countries have highlighted the need for external financial support to achieve their climate goals, and nature bonds provide a vehicle for channeling such resources. With the backing of multilateral development banks, development finance institutions, or donor governments, nature bonds can attract private investment into projects aligned with NDCs. This mobilization of blended finance helps bridge the gap between domestic resources and the scale of investment needed to achieve national targets.

The social dimensions of NDCs are equally important, and nature bonds can be structured to support them. Many NDCs emphasize co-benefits such as job creation, poverty reduction, and the protection of indigenous rights. By incorporating social indicators into their frameworks, nature bonds ensure that financed projects contribute not only to ecological outcomes but also to inclusive development. This alignment strengthens the political and social legitimacy of NDC implementation while demonstrating that climate action can deliver broad-based benefits.

Policy innovation is another area where nature bonds intersect with NDCs. Governments can design regulatory frameworks that integrate nature bonds into national financing strategies, creating synergies between public and private finance. For example, proceeds from sovereign nature bonds can be earmarked for projects directly tied to NDC commitments, while tax incentives can encourage private issuances aligned with national priorities. These policy measures create coherence between climate planning and financial markets, increasing the likelihood that NDCs are achieved.

Nature bonds also provide a means for countries to demonstrate leadership on the international stage. Issuing a nature bond signals a commitment to innovative climate finance and can enhance a country's reputation in global climate negotiations. This signaling effect can attract further investment and strengthen partnerships with donors and development institutions. For countries seeking to raise ambition in their NDCs, the ability to demonstrate access to credible, scalable financing instruments is a powerful enabler.

The link between nature bonds and NDCs is not only financial but also strategic. By structuring financing around measurable outcomes, governments gain a tool for prioritizing and sequencing climate actions. Bond frameworks encourage careful project selection, rigorous monitoring, and transparent reporting, all of which contribute to stronger NDC implementation. The discipline imposed by capital markets can therefore complement policy planning, reinforcing the credibility and effectiveness of national climate strategies.

Through these multiple dimensions—mobilizing mitigation and adaptation finance, integrating with national strategies, enhancing transparency, unlocking international capital, supporting social co-benefits, and strengthening policy coherence—nature bonds directly support the realization of NDC commitments. They provide governments with a mechanism to translate international climate goals into actionable financing pathways while offering investors confidence that their capital contributes to globally recognized priorities.

Enhancing Climate Resilience Through Nature-Based Solutions

NBS have emerged as a cornerstone of strategies to enhance climate resilience. They emphasize working with natural systems rather than against them, leveraging ecosystems' inherent capacity to buffer climate impacts and sustain livelihoods. Within the framework of nature bonds, financing NBS creates opportunities to scale up these interventions, linking capital markets with ecological resilience. The alignment of bond structures with ecosystem outcomes ensures that financing flows contribute directly to building adaptive capacity while maintaining ecological integrity.

One of the most widely recognized contributions of NBS to climate resilience is their role in protecting against extreme weather events. Coastal ecosystems such as mangroves, coral reefs, and salt marshes act as natural barriers, reducing storm surges and mitigating coastal erosion. Forests and wetlands regulate water flows, reducing flood risk during heavy rains and maintaining water availability during droughts. By financing restoration and protection of these ecosystems, nature bonds can strengthen natural defenses that reduce vulnerability for communities, infrastructure, and economies. The financial linkage between bond repayment and verified ecological outcomes ensures that these protective functions are preserved and enhanced over time.

NBS also support food and water security, which are increasingly threatened by climate variability. Sustainable land management practices such as agroforestry, soil conservation, and watershed protection improve agricultural resilience by maintaining soil fertility, reducing erosion, and ensuring reliable water supplies. Forested watersheds act as natural filtration systems, safeguarding clean water sources even as climate pressures intensify. When nature bonds finance these interventions, they provide long-term benefits that extend beyond immediate ecological gains, reinforcing the resilience of human systems dependent on ecosystem services.

Biodiversity conservation is another pathway through which NBS enhance resilience. Diverse ecosystems are inherently more resilient to climate shocks, as species and habitats provide functional redundancy and adaptability. For example, diverse forests can recover more quickly from disturbances, while varied agricultural landscapes are less susceptible to pests and diseases exacerbated by changing climates. Financing through nature bonds supports the maintenance of biodiversity as a resilience asset, ensuring that ecosystems retain their adaptive capacity under uncertain climate futures.

The integration of NBS into urban systems demonstrates their versatility in enhancing resilience. Cities are increasingly vulnerable to heat waves, flooding, and other climate-related hazards. Urban green spaces, permeable surfaces, and restored rivers reduce heat island effects, absorb stormwater, and improve air quality. Nature bonds issued by municipalities can fund such interventions, embedding resilience directly into urban planning. By tying financial performance to ecological outcomes, these bonds ensure that urban NBS deliver measurable and sustained benefits for climate adaptation.

Social resilience is strengthened when NBS are financed effectively. Communities that rely on ecosystems for livelihoods, such as fishing, farming, or forestry, gain adaptive capacity when ecosystems are conserved or restored. Participatory approaches to NBS ensure that local knowledge and needs are incorporated into project design, fostering ownership and long-term sustainability. Nature bonds that embed social safeguards and benefit-sharing mechanisms provide an avenue for ensuring that resilience-building efforts are inclusive and equitable, reinforcing the social dimensions of adaptation.

Verification and monitoring systems play a central role in ensuring that NBS financed through nature bonds genuinely enhance resilience. Ecological indicators such as restored mangrove cover, improved soil moisture, or increased species diversity can serve as measurable benchmarks. Independent verification ensures credibility, providing investors with assurance that financed projects deliver real adaptation benefits. Advances in satellite monitoring, drone technologies, and data analytics enhance the ability to track resilience outcomes over time, strengthening the link between financial and ecological performance.

The scalability of NBS depends in part on their integration into national adaptation plans and climate strategies. Many countries include NBS as key elements of their NDCs under the Paris Agreement, recognizing their cost-effectiveness and co-benefits. Nature bonds provide a financing vehicle to operationalize these commitments, channeling private and public capital into NBS at a scale commensurate with national climate goals. By embedding repayment conditions tied to NBS outcomes, bonds ensure that financing is directly linked to strengthening climate resilience.

Economic considerations also highlight the value of financing NBS through bonds. Traditional infrastructure designed to address climate risks often requires large upfront investments and can degrade over time. By contrast, NBS often provide increasing benefits as ecosystems mature and regenerate. For example, restored mangroves not only protect coasts but also support fisheries and carbon sequestration. Financing these interventions through nature bonds aligns long-term ecological and financial value, as both resilience and returns can grow over the life of the instrument.

Investor confidence in resilience-focused nature bonds is supported by the growing recognition of climate-related risks in financial markets. Asset managers and institutional investors are increasingly aware that climate change poses material risks to portfolios. Instruments that finance NBS provide a way to hedge against these risks while demonstrating alignment with climate adaptation goals. By enhancing transparency and tying financial terms to resilience outcomes, nature bonds offer a credible means for investors to participate in climate adaptation at scale.

The ability of NBS to generate multiple co-benefits strengthens their appeal as targets for bond financing. Beyond climate resilience, NBS contribute to biodiversity protection, carbon sequestration, cultural values, and community well-being. Financing mechanisms that capture these multifaceted benefits create stronger cases for investment. Nature bonds are particularly well-suited to this role, as their structures can be designed to reflect the multiple outcomes of NBS, reinforcing their alignment with broad sustainability objectives while focusing on resilience.

Through their integration of ecological performance into financial systems, nature bonds provide a scalable pathway to fund NBS that strengthen resilience across diverse geographies and sectors. By linking capital markets with nature's adaptive capacities, they create mechanisms that both safeguard ecosystems and support communities facing climate challenges.

Chapter 5: Nature Bonds and Biodiversity Frameworks

Nature bonds intersect directly with global biodiversity frameworks that aim to halt and reverse ecosystem degradation while ensuring sustainable use of natural resources. By embedding ecological performance into financial instruments, they translate high-level policy commitments into measurable outcomes on the ground. This chapter examines how nature bonds align with the Kunming-Montreal Global Biodiversity Framework and related international agreements, highlighting their role in financing conservation, restoration, and sustainable resource management. It also considers the importance of standardized indicators, transparent reporting, and global cooperation in ensuring that nature bonds contribute meaningfully to biodiversity protection targets.

The Kunming-Montreal Global Biodiversity Framework

The Kunming-Montreal Global Biodiversity Framework (GBF), adopted in December 2022 at the 15th Conference of the Parties (COP15) to the Convention on Biological Diversity, provides the central global roadmap for halting and reversing biodiversity loss by 2030 and ensuring nature's recovery by mid-century. The framework emerged from recognition that existing commitments had fallen short of addressing the accelerating decline of ecosystems, habitats, and species worldwide. It builds on earlier biodiversity strategies but introduces more ambitious targets, clearer accountability measures, and stronger integration with climate and sustainable development agendas.

The GBF sets out four overarching goals for 2050, complemented by 23 targets for 2030. The goals emphasize maintaining ecosystem integrity, halting species extinctions, ensuring fair and equitable benefit-sharing from the use of genetic resources, and mobilizing adequate financial resources. The 23 targets translate these aspirations into actionable measures, such as conserving at least 30 percent of land and ocean areas, restoring degraded ecosystems, reducing pollution harmful to biodiversity, and eliminating harmful subsidies. These targets are designed to be measurable and time-bound, addressing the shortcomings of previous biodiversity frameworks that suffered from vague or aspirational goals.

For nature bonds, the GBF provides a globally recognized framework that links financing to tangible conservation outcomes. Issuers can design bond structures that align with specific GBF targets, such as restoring wetlands, expanding protected areas, or reducing nutrient runoff into rivers and oceans. By doing so, they situate their instruments within a broader international agenda, providing investors with assurance that financed projects contribute to globally agreed objectives. The GBF thus serves as both a guiding reference and a legitimizing force for the development of nature bonds.

A core strength of the GBF is its emphasis on measurable indicators. Unlike earlier biodiversity frameworks, the Kunming-Montreal agreement outlines mechanisms for monitoring progress through standardized reporting and transparency requirements. Each country is expected to submit national biodiversity strategies and action plans consistent with the framework, as well as periodic progress reports. This emphasis on accountability aligns directly with the outcome-based nature of nature bonds. Both rely on clear, verifiable indicators to demonstrate progress and maintain credibility with stakeholders.

The GBF also underscores the importance of mobilizing financial resources at an unprecedented scale. It calls for increasing biodiversity-related financing from all sources—public, private, domestic, and international—to at least $200 billion annually by 2030. It also emphasizes redirecting or reforming subsidies harmful to biodiversity, estimated at hundreds of billions of dollars each year. Nature bonds provide one pathway to operationalize this financial ambition, mobilizing private capital in ways that complement public and philanthropic funding. By tying financial returns to GBF-aligned outcomes, nature bonds directly contribute to the framework's financing goals.

Equity and inclusivity are central themes of the GBF. The framework emphasizes the role of indigenous peoples and local communities, recognizing their stewardship of biodiversity and the need to respect their rights. It also highlights equitable sharing of benefits derived from genetic resources. For nature bonds, this creates an imperative to incorporate social safeguards and benefit-sharing mechanisms. Instruments that finance conservation in ways that exclude or disempower local communities would conflict with the GBF's principles. Aligning bond structures with the framework therefore requires careful attention to equity, participation, and inclusivity alongside ecological outcomes.

The integration of the GBF with other global agendas, including the Paris Agreement and the Sustainable Development Goals, enhances its relevance for nature bonds. Climate change and biodiversity loss are deeply interconnected, and the GBF acknowledges the role of healthy ecosystems in climate mitigation and adaptation. Nature bonds designed to support reforestation, coastal restoration, or sustainable agriculture contribute not only to biodiversity targets but also to climate resilience and carbon sequestration. This creates opportunities for bonds to align with multiple frameworks simultaneously, increasing their appeal to investors seeking integrated sustainability outcomes.

Monitoring and reporting under the GBF provide a platform for strengthening investor confidence in nature bonds. The framework's call for standardized indicators and transparent reporting supports the development of comparable metrics across issuances, reducing fragmentation and uncertainty in the market. As countries build systems to monitor progress toward GBF targets, issuers can draw on these systems to verify bond outcomes, creating synergies between national reporting obligations and investor assurance needs.

The GBF's ambition to conserve 30 percent of land and ocean by 2030—often referred to as the "30x30" target—has become one of its most prominent commitments. This target in particular offers opportunities for nature bonds to play a catalytic role. Financing for protected area expansion, ecosystem corridors, and marine conservation can be structured into bond frameworks, linking capital flows to progress toward 30x30. By embedding this target into financial instruments, issuers help operationalize a flagship element of the GBF while providing investors with clear, measurable objectives.

Through its emphasis on ambitious, measurable targets, accountability mechanisms, financing mobilization, and equity, the Kunming-Montreal Global Biodiversity Framework provides the global context within which nature bonds can be designed, issued, and scaled. It offers both the policy legitimacy and the operational guidance needed to ensure that these instruments deliver real biodiversity outcomes while complementing broader sustainability agendas.

Financing Protected Areas and Ecosystem Restoration

Protected areas and ecosystem restoration projects are among the most critical pathways for addressing biodiversity loss, strengthening climate resilience, and safeguarding ecosystem services essential to human well-being. However, financing these efforts has historically fallen short of what is needed. Nature bonds provide a promising mechanism to close this gap by mobilizing large-scale capital and directing it toward conservation and restoration outcomes that align with international biodiversity and climate goals.

Protected areas form the cornerstone of biodiversity conservation strategies worldwide. They secure habitats for species, preserve ecosystem functions, and protect natural resources that underpin livelihoods and cultural values. Yet, many protected areas face chronic underfunding, leading to challenges in management, enforcement, and community engagement. Traditional funding sources, such as government budgets and international grants, are often inadequate and subject to political and economic fluctuations. By issuing nature bonds linked to the performance of protected areas, governments and organizations can establish more reliable streams of capital. Proceeds can finance infrastructure, ranger programs, ecological monitoring, and community development initiatives tied to conservation outcomes.

Ecosystem restoration complements protected area financing by repairing degraded landscapes and reviving ecological functions. Global commitments such as the UN Decade on Ecosystem Restoration and the Kunming-Montreal Global Biodiversity Framework highlight restoration as a key strategy for reversing biodiversity decline and addressing climate change. Restoration projects can range from reforestation and wetland rehabilitation to soil regeneration and coral reef recovery. Financing these efforts through nature bonds creates opportunities for long-term, outcome-based investment. Investors are assured that their capital contributes to measurable increases in ecosystem health, such as improved vegetation cover, enhanced carbon storage, or restored hydrological balance.

Nature bonds can be structured in various ways to support conservation and restoration. Sovereign or sub-sovereign issuances provide governments with capital to expand and maintain protected area networks. Corporate or development finance-backed bonds can focus on restoration initiatives linked to supply chains, water security, or carbon markets. The inclusion of performance-linked repayment terms further strengthens accountability, ensuring that financial benefits are tied to verifiable ecological improvements. This design helps overcome one of the main criticisms of conservation finance—that funds are not always used efficiently or transparently.

One of the key strengths of financing through nature bonds is the ability to integrate social and ecological outcomes. Protected areas and restoration projects often affect communities living in or near ecosystems. Bonds can incorporate benefit-sharing mechanisms, financing programs that support sustainable livelihoods, healthcare, or education alongside conservation. This integration helps secure community support for conservation measures, reducing conflict and enhancing long-term sustainability. Investors gain confidence knowing that financed projects deliver not only ecological but also social returns, broadening the appeal of the bonds to impact-focused capital.

Independent monitoring and verification systems play an essential role in ensuring that financing for protected areas and restoration achieves its intended outcomes. Satellite imagery, ecological surveys, and biodiversity indicators provide credible evidence of progress. These tools allow issuers to report transparently to investors, reinforcing trust in the bond mechanism. Verified outcomes also contribute to international reporting frameworks, helping countries demonstrate progress toward biodiversity and climate commitments.

The scaling potential of nature bonds for protected areas and restoration is significant. Global targets such as protecting 30 percent of land and oceans by 2030 and restoring degraded ecosystems require unprecedented levels of financing. Nature bonds provide a scalable solution by tapping into private capital markets, complementing traditional sources of funding. Their adaptability to different contexts—sovereign, municipal, or corporate—enables them to be tailored to national strategies or local priorities.

By channeling investment into protected areas and ecosystem restoration, nature bonds create durable benefits that extend across ecological, social, and economic dimensions. They enhance biodiversity, increase resilience to climate impacts, secure ecosystem services such as clean water and fertile soils, and strengthen local communities. Through innovative structuring, transparent monitoring, and alignment with global frameworks, nature bonds represent a critical pathway to mobilize the resources needed for conservation and restoration at scale.

Supporting Indigenous and Local Community Rights

Indigenous peoples and local communities play a central role in the stewardship of ecosystems, often managing some of the most biodiverse and ecologically significant areas on the planet. Their knowledge, practices, and cultural values contribute to sustaining landscapes and seascapes that are critical for climate resilience, biodiversity protection, and the provision of ecosystem services. Yet, despite their importance, these communities frequently face marginalization in decision-making processes and limited access to financial resources that shape conservation and climate initiatives. Nature bonds, when designed responsibly, can help address these challenges by embedding the protection and empowerment of indigenous and local community rights within their frameworks.

A fundamental principle for supporting indigenous and local rights through nature bonds is the recognition of land tenure and resource access. Secure land rights are essential for communities to continue their stewardship practices and to benefit from conservation finance. Bonds that channel investment into conservation or restoration must therefore be structured to uphold, not undermine, the tenure rights of local stakeholders. This requires rigorous due diligence, legal safeguards, and participatory governance structures to ensure that bond proceeds are invested in ways that strengthen community ownership rather than displace or disenfranchise people.

Free, prior, and informed consent (FPIC) is another cornerstone of community rights that must be respected in the design of nature bonds. FPIC ensures that indigenous and local communities are meaningfully consulted and have the ability to approve or reject projects that affect their territories, livelihoods, and cultural heritage. Incorporating FPIC into bond frameworks provides legitimacy and reduces the risk of conflict or reputational harm for issuers and investors. Transparent processes for consultation, co-design, and decision-making help build trust between communities, governments, and financial institutions, laying the foundation for long-term success.

Nature bonds can also provide a platform for channeling financial benefits directly to communities. Conservation and restoration projects often generate revenues through ecosystem services, tourism, or carbon credits. Bond structures that incorporate benefit-sharing mechanisms ensure that a fair portion of these revenues flows back to communities, supporting livelihoods, education, healthcare, and cultural preservation. By embedding equitable distribution of benefits into repayment structures or project financing plans, issuers enhance both the social and ecological outcomes of the bond.

Local and traditional knowledge systems are invaluable for achieving conservation and climate outcomes, and nature bonds can be designed to integrate this knowledge. Indigenous practices in sustainable land management, water governance, and biodiversity monitoring often complement scientific approaches. Embedding community participation in monitoring and verification processes not only strengthens accountability but also validates the role of local knowledge in global sustainability efforts. This integration demonstrates respect for cultural heritage while improving the ecological credibility of financed projects.

Transparency and accountability mechanisms must be adapted to include community perspectives. Independent verification of ecological outcomes should be complemented by participatory monitoring that empowers communities to track the impacts of projects in their territories. Accessible reporting formats and mechanisms for grievance redress are essential to ensure that community voices are heard and that any adverse impacts are promptly addressed. Such mechanisms strengthen investor confidence by demonstrating that social risks are being managed alongside ecological and financial performance.

Capacity building is another avenue through which nature bonds can support indigenous and local rights. Many communities face barriers to participating fully in conservation finance due to limited technical expertise or institutional support. Bonds that allocate resources for training, institutional strengthening, and capacity building enable communities to take an active role in project governance and financial management. Empowering local institutions ensures that communities can sustain conservation outcomes beyond the lifetime of individual bond issuances.

Collaboration with civil society organizations, non-governmental organizations, and multilateral agencies further enhances the ability of nature bonds to support community rights. These actors can serve as intermediaries, providing technical assistance, facilitating dialogue, and ensuring that community priorities are represented in project design. Their involvement can also improve accountability, as independent organizations can monitor whether issuers are upholding commitments to indigenous and local rights.

Aligning nature bonds with international frameworks strengthens their legitimacy in protecting community rights. The United Nations Declaration on the Rights of Indigenous Peoples, International Labour Organization Convention 169, and the safeguards of multilateral development banks all provide standards for ensuring respect for rights and participation. By explicitly referencing and integrating these frameworks, issuers can demonstrate alignment with recognized global norms, reassuring investors and stakeholders that social dimensions are being addressed with seriousness and rigor.

Supporting indigenous and local community rights through nature bonds also enhances ecological effectiveness. Communities with secure rights and adequate resources are more likely to engage in long-term stewardship of ecosystems, ensuring durability of conservation outcomes. Studies have shown that areas managed by indigenous peoples often have equal or better conservation results compared to state-managed protected areas. By directing capital into rights-based approaches, nature bonds leverage this stewardship to achieve measurable ecological impact, aligning social justice with environmental goals.

The intersection of finance and rights requires careful balance. Poorly designed instruments risk replicating historical injustices by centralizing control and excluding communities. Well-designed nature bonds, in contrast, recognize that conservation and climate resilience cannot be achieved without the active participation and empowerment of those who live closest to nature. By embedding rights into the financial architecture of bonds—through tenure recognition, FPIC, benefit-sharing, participatory monitoring, capacity building, and alignment with global standards—nature bonds can provide a pathway for financing that respects and strengthens the role of indigenous and local communities.

Chapter 6: Market Development and Investor Demand

The long-term success of nature bonds depends on the creation of robust markets and the ability to attract sustained investor demand. Market development requires credible standards, transparent reporting systems, and sufficient liquidity to make nature bonds competitive with other sustainable finance instruments. At the same time, investor interest is shaped by perceptions of risk, return, and the credibility of ecological outcomes. This chapter explores the dynamics of market growth, the evolving preferences of institutional investors, sovereign wealth funds, and private capital, and the mechanisms needed to build confidence, scale issuance, and expand participation across global markets.

The Evolution of ESG Investing

ESG investing has undergone a profound transformation over the past several decades, evolving from niche strategies focused on ethical exclusions to a mainstream approach that shapes global capital markets. Its trajectory reflects changing societal expectations, growing awareness of systemic risks, and recognition that long-term financial performance is inseparable from environmental and social factors. Understanding the evolution of ESG investing provides critical context for instruments such as nature bonds, which represent the latest wave of innovation within sustainable finance.

The origins of ESG investing can be traced to socially responsible investing (SRI) in the 1960s and 1970s. During this period, faith-based groups, labor unions, and activist investors began to screen investments to avoid companies involved in activities they deemed unethical, such as tobacco, weapons, or apartheid South Africa. This exclusionary approach focused on aligning investments with moral or ethical values, often at the cost of reduced diversification and potentially lower financial returns. While limited in scale, SRI laid the groundwork by demonstrating that investor preferences could extend beyond purely financial considerations.

The 1990s marked a turning point with the integration of environmental and social issues into broader risk management frameworks. Growing evidence of climate change, corporate scandals, and globalization's social impacts created pressure for investors to consider a wider set of non-financial factors. The term "ESG" began to gain traction in the early 2000s, popularized by initiatives such as the United Nations Principles for Responsible Investment (PRI), launched in 2006. The PRI encouraged institutional investors to incorporate ESG factors into their decision-making processes, signaling a shift from values-driven exclusion to risk-adjusted integration. ESG was increasingly framed not as a moral choice but as a means of identifying material risks and opportunities.

As ESG matured, it expanded beyond risk mitigation to value creation. Investors began to recognize that companies with strong ESG performance often exhibited operational efficiencies, enhanced brand reputation, and better governance practices, all of which contributed to long-term financial resilience. Empirical studies provided evidence that ESG integration could enhance returns or reduce volatility, reinforcing its legitimacy as a financial strategy. Asset managers began to launch ESG-focused funds, and indices such as the Dow Jones Sustainability Index and MSCI ESG ratings provided benchmarks that further mainstreamed the practice.

The 2010s witnessed rapid growth and diversification in ESG strategies. Climate change became a dominant theme, with investors increasingly scrutinizing carbon footprints, energy transitions, and stranded asset risks. Governance failures such as corruption scandals and financial crises further underscored the importance of strong oversight structures. Social issues, including labor rights, diversity, and community relations, also gained prominence, particularly as globalization highlighted inequities in supply chains. This decade saw ESG move from the margins to the mainstream, with trillions of dollars flowing into ESG-related funds and mandates. Institutional investors such as pension funds and sovereign wealth funds began to make ESG integration a default expectation rather than an optional strategy.

Policy and regulatory developments accelerated this evolution. Governments and financial regulators introduced disclosure requirements and taxonomies to standardize ESG reporting. The European Union's Sustainable Finance Disclosure Regulation (SFDR) and the development of green and sustainable taxonomies created frameworks for greater transparency and comparability. International initiatives, such as the Task Force on Climate-related Financial Disclosures (TCFD), established guidelines for reporting climate risks, further embedding ESG into financial systems. These regulatory shifts signaled that ESG considerations were no longer optional but integral to fiduciary duty and long-term portfolio resilience.

Investor demand also evolved during this period, with younger generations of investors placing greater emphasis on sustainability and impact. The rise of passive investing and exchange-traded funds (ETFs) created demand for ESG indices that allowed investors to align their portfolios with environmental and social goals without sacrificing diversification. This democratization of ESG investing broadened participation beyond institutional investors, embedding sustainability considerations across retail markets as well.

Despite its growth, ESG investing has faced challenges and criticism. Skeptics argue that ESG ratings lack consistency, with methodologies varying widely among providers. Concerns about greenwashing—where companies exaggerate or misrepresent their sustainability performance—have raised questions about the credibility of ESG claims. Some critics also argue that ESG investing can dilute focus by attempting to address too many issues at once, making it difficult to measure tangible outcomes. These criticisms have prompted calls for greater standardization, accountability, and outcome-based metrics in ESG frameworks.

The most recent phase of ESG evolution emphasizes impact and outcomes. Investors are increasingly seeking evidence that their capital contributes to real-world environmental and social improvements, not just improved scores or reduced portfolio risks. This has led to the growth of impact investing, sustainability-linked instruments, and thematic finance products such as green bonds, blue bonds, and nature bonds. ESG is no longer just about screening or integration but about driving measurable progress toward global sustainability goals.

The future trajectory of ESG investing points toward deeper integration with systemic risk management and alignment with international frameworks such as the Paris Agreement and the Kunming-Montreal Global Biodiversity Framework. As climate change, biodiversity loss, and social inequality intensify, investors are recognizing that financial markets cannot remain insulated from these global challenges. ESG is increasingly seen as a mechanism for aligning capital flows with long-term sustainability, reinforcing its role as a core component of modern finance.

The evolution of ESG investing—from exclusionary screens to risk integration, value creation, and outcome-based impact—illustrates how investor priorities and societal expectations have reshaped finance over time. Each stage of this evolution has expanded the scope and legitimacy of sustainability considerations within capital markets, laying the foundation for innovative instruments like nature bonds that directly tie financial performance to ecological and social outcomes.

Institutional Investors and Sovereign Wealth Funds

Institutional investors and sovereign wealth funds (SWFs) are increasingly important actors in the growth and mainstreaming of nature bonds. With their vast pools of capital, long-term investment horizons, and influence over market norms, these investors are uniquely positioned to drive the integration of biodiversity and ecosystem considerations into global finance. Their participation not only mobilizes significant funding for conservation and restoration but also signals credibility and stability to broader financial markets.

Institutional investors—such as pension funds, insurance companies, and asset managers—are motivated to engage with nature bonds for several reasons. A growing recognition of ESG risks has pushed these institutions to reassess their portfolios, as biodiversity loss and ecosystem degradation pose material financial threats. For example, disruptions to supply chains, water scarcity, or climate-related damages can undermine long-term asset performance. Nature bonds provide a direct vehicle for mitigating such risks by channeling capital into projects that enhance ecological resilience. By aligning their investments with ecosystem outcomes, institutional investors address systemic risks while responding to rising client and stakeholder demands for sustainability.

The long-term orientation of pension funds and insurers makes them particularly suited to nature bonds. Conservation and restoration projects often span decades, with ecological benefits accruing gradually. Institutional investors accustomed to managing liabilities over similar timeframes can align with these horizons, matching long-term obligations to investments that provide enduring ecological and financial returns. This compatibility between time horizons strengthens the case for integrating nature bonds into institutional portfolios.

Another factor driving institutional investor participation is the demand for diversification within sustainable finance. As green bond markets expand, investors are seeking opportunities to broaden their exposure to sustainability-linked instruments. Nature bonds, with their focus on biodiversity and ecosystem services, complement existing allocations to climate and energy transitions. They offer investors the chance to address underfunded areas of sustainability while diversifying portfolio risks. This differentiation enhances the attractiveness of nature bonds as a distinct asset class within the ESG investment universe.

Sovereign wealth funds play a particularly strategic role. Managing trillions of dollars in assets globally, SWFs are often linked to resource-rich countries whose economies depend heavily on natural capital. These funds are increasingly recognizing the importance of aligning their portfolios with sustainability goals to secure long-term national wealth. Nature bonds provide a way for SWFs to invest in preserving the very ecosystems that underpin economic stability, such as forests, fisheries, and watersheds. By doing so, they align financial strategies with national priorities in biodiversity and climate resilience.

SWFs also carry significant signaling power. Their participation in nature bond markets can attract other institutional investors, creating momentum and scaling opportunities. When sovereign wealth funds commit capital to biodiversity-linked instruments, they not only mobilize large sums directly but also demonstrate confidence in the credibility of these markets. This signaling effect helps reduce perceived risk and accelerates mainstream adoption of nature bonds across global finance.

The integration of nature bonds into institutional and sovereign wealth portfolios also reflects evolving regulatory and policy frameworks. Many jurisdictions now require large investors to disclose nature-related risks and align with international commitments such as the Paris Agreement and the Kunming-Montreal Global Biodiversity Framework. Institutional investors and SWFs that allocate to nature bonds can demonstrate compliance with these obligations while showcasing leadership in sustainable finance. This regulatory alignment further reinforces the credibility and attractiveness of nature bonds.

Collaboration between institutional investors, SWFs, and MDBs enhances the effectiveness of nature bond financing. MDBs often provide credit enhancements, guarantees, or technical assistance that de-risk investments for large institutional players. By partnering with MDBs, institutional investors and SWFs can participate in nature bonds with greater confidence, knowing that governance structures and monitoring systems are in place. These partnerships also facilitate the flow of capital to emerging markets, where financing needs for conservation and restoration are greatest.

Investor confidence in nature bonds is further strengthened by transparency and verification mechanisms. Institutional investors and SWFs require robust data to assess both financial performance and ecological impact. Independent monitoring and reporting systems, coupled with adherence to international standards, provide the accountability these investors demand. When issuers demonstrate measurable outcomes aligned with biodiversity frameworks, institutional investors are more likely to view nature bonds as credible, scalable, and suitable for mainstream portfolios.

Social and reputational considerations also influence institutional and sovereign wealth fund engagement. Both types of investors are under increasing scrutiny from civil society, beneficiaries, and the public to demonstrate responsible investment practices. Allocating to nature bonds allows them to showcase alignment with global sustainability goals, strengthening legitimacy and reputation. This reputational benefit complements financial and risk-management motivations, creating a multi-faceted rationale for engagement.

The scale of capital managed by institutional investors and SWFs means that even modest allocations to nature bonds can have transformative effects. By anchoring issuances, these investors provide stability, attract additional participants, and create benchmarks for pricing and performance. Their involvement supports market development, helping nature bonds transition from niche instruments to mainstream tools for financing biodiversity and ecosystem restoration.

Building Scalable and Liquid Markets for Nature Bonds

For nature bonds to become a mainstream component of sustainable finance, they must transition from small, bespoke issuances to scalable and liquid markets capable of attracting diverse investors. Liquidity, standardization, and scale are essential conditions for mobilizing the trillions of dollars required to close biodiversity and conservation finance gaps. Building such markets requires careful design, robust governance, and alignment with both investor expectations and ecological imperatives.

Scalability begins with the creation of standardized frameworks. Early issuances of nature bonds have often been project-specific, customized to local contexts, and relatively small in size. While such pilots demonstrate feasibility, they do not easily lend themselves to replication at scale. Establishing common standards for eligibility, use of proceeds, ecological metrics, and reporting would allow issuers to structure bonds in ways that are recognizable and comparable across markets. Frameworks modeled on the Green Bond Principles or sustainability taxonomies can provide this consistency, ensuring that investors have clarity on what qualifies as a nature bond and how performance is measured.

Standardization also supports aggregation. Conservation and restoration projects are often fragmented, with limited financial capacity to issue bonds independently. By aggregating smaller projects into portfolios that meet standardized criteria, issuers can achieve the scale necessary to attract institutional investors. Pooled nature bond structures, similar to asset-backed securities, could package multiple projects together, spreading risk and increasing investable volume. This approach also reduces transaction costs, which are often a barrier to scaling conservation finance.

Liquidity is another critical factor. Investors require the ability to buy and sell instruments without excessive cost or delay. Currently, many sustainability-linked instruments, including nature bonds, are held to maturity, limiting secondary market activity. Building liquidity requires creating benchmarks, indices, and trading platforms that allow for price discovery and comparability. Sovereign and large corporate issuances can play an anchoring role by creating sizable, widely traded instruments that set standards for the broader market. Once benchmarks are established, smaller issuances can align with them, gradually building depth and liquidity.

The role of sovereign issuances is particularly significant for scalability and liquidity. Sovereign nature bonds backed by national governments can be issued in large volumes, creating benchmark instruments that attract institutional investors. These issuances also provide signaling power, demonstrating governmental commitment to biodiversity and climate goals. By setting precedents for structure, transparency, and reporting, sovereign bonds create a template that can be replicated at sub-sovereign, corporate, or community levels. The establishment of sovereign benchmarks is often a catalyst for broader market development, as seen in the growth of green bond markets.

Market infrastructure is equally important. Exchanges, clearing systems, and rating agencies must adapt to accommodate nature bonds. Listing requirements should incorporate sustainability disclosures, while rating methodologies must integrate ecological performance alongside traditional credit analysis. Dedicated indices tracking nature bond performance would increase visibility and attract passive investment flows through ETFs and other vehicles. These elements create the ecosystem necessary for liquid and scalable markets.

Technology can accelerate the development of scalable markets. Digital platforms enable the tokenization of nature bonds, breaking them into smaller units that can be traded more easily, expanding access to retail investors, and improving liquidity. Blockchain applications can embed ecological performance metrics into smart contracts, automating coupon adjustments or repayment terms based on verified outcomes. Such innovations reduce transaction costs, increase transparency, and foster trust, all of which are essential for market expansion.

Blended finance plays a crucial role in enabling scalability. Many conservation projects are perceived as high-risk due to ecological uncertainty, political instability, or long time horizons. Public and philanthropic capital can provide credit enhancements, guarantees, or first-loss capital that reduce risks for private investors. By lowering barriers to entry, blended structures attract larger pools of capital, allowing markets to grow. As confidence builds, reliance on concessional support can decrease, paving the way for more purely commercial issuances.

Global policy frameworks provide a supportive backdrop for scaling markets. The Kunming-Montreal Global Biodiversity Framework and the Paris Agreement both highlight the need for massive increases in conservation finance. By aligning nature bond structures with these frameworks, issuers can tap into growing investor demand for instruments that demonstrate policy coherence. MDBs and DFIs can further support scalability by providing technical assistance, co-investment, and risk-sharing mechanisms. Their participation reassures investors and helps standardize practices across regions.

Capacity building among issuers and investors is also essential. Many potential issuers, particularly in developing countries, lack the technical expertise to design and manage nature bond programs. Training, technical assistance, and knowledge-sharing platforms can address this gap, enabling a wider range of actors to participate in the market. On the investor side, increased awareness and education about the financial and ecological characteristics of nature bonds are needed to build demand. As knowledge spreads, investor bases diversify, contributing to market depth and liquidity.

Transparency and accountability underpin market credibility. Scalable markets depend on robust systems for monitoring, reporting, and verification of ecological outcomes. Without credible data, investors will hesitate to commit large volumes of capital. Independent verification, standardized reporting frameworks, and integration of advanced monitoring technologies ensure that markets remain trustworthy as they grow. Transparency also fosters comparability, enabling investors to assess relative performance and make informed allocation decisions.

The integration of nature bonds into mainstream financial portfolios is a critical milestone for liquidity. Once asset managers, pension funds, and sovereign wealth funds begin to treat nature bonds as core holdings rather than niche products, markets can expand rapidly. Inclusion in sustainable finance indices, alignment with disclosure requirements, and recognition by regulators as credible instruments all facilitate this integration. As demand grows, issuers gain confidence to scale up, creating a virtuous cycle of supply and demand that reinforces market liquidity.

Regional cooperation can also support scalability. Biodiversity challenges often cross borders, requiring coordinated financing solutions. Regional platforms for issuing pooled nature bonds can reduce costs, spread risk, and create larger instruments that appeal to global investors. For example, transboundary watershed or forest conservation initiatives could be financed through regional bond programs, enhancing both ecological effectiveness and market scale.

The path to building scalable and liquid markets for nature bonds requires a combination of standardization, sovereign leadership, technological innovation, blended finance, capacity building, and transparency. Each element reinforces the others, creating the conditions for nature bonds to evolve from experimental instruments into mainstream tools for financing biodiversity and ecosystem resilience. By embedding ecological performance into financial systems while ensuring market efficiency, scalable and liquid nature bond markets can mobilize capital at the scale necessary to meet global conservation and climate goals.

Chapter 7: Challenges and Risks

The expansion of nature bonds faces significant hurdles that must be addressed to secure their long-term viability. While these instruments promise to align financial flows with ecological outcomes, they are exposed to a range of financial, political, and operational risks. Challenges include the potential for greenwashing, high transaction costs, uncertain ecological performance, and limited market liquidity. Political instability, weak governance frameworks, and inconsistent global standards further complicate development. This chapter examines the risks that threaten credibility and investor confidence, highlighting the importance of transparency, oversight, and robust safeguards in ensuring that nature bonds deliver genuine environmental impact.

Risk of Greenwashing and Mislabeling

The credibility of nature bonds, like other instruments in sustainable finance, depends heavily on the ability to demonstrate genuine ecological impact. A central challenge in this regard is the risk of greenwashing and mislabeling. Greenwashing occurs when issuers exaggerate, misrepresent, or falsely claim environmental benefits to attract investment, while mislabeling involves categorizing financial products as "green" or "nature-focused" when they do not align with established sustainability criteria. Both issues undermine investor confidence, dilute the effectiveness of conservation finance, and threaten the legitimacy of the broader sustainable finance market.

One source of greenwashing risk in nature bonds stems from vague or poorly defined use-of-proceeds criteria. If issuers fail to clearly specify how funds will be used, investors may be misled into believing that their capital supports conservation outcomes when it is directed toward projects with marginal or indirect ecological benefits. For example, projects framed as biodiversity-friendly may, in practice, prioritize infrastructure with limited or no positive impact on ecosystems. Without strict guidelines, issuers can label bonds as nature-related while pursuing activities that do not deliver measurable improvements.

A related challenge lies in the selection of indicators used to measure outcomes. Nature bonds are often tied to ecological metrics such as restored hectares, reduced deforestation, or improved water quality. However, when indicators are not scientifically robust, independently verifiable, or aligned with broader ecological priorities, they open the door to misrepresentation. Overly simplistic or narrow metrics may fail to capture the complexity of ecosystem health, allowing issuers to claim success based on limited improvements that mask broader environmental decline.

The lack of harmonized standards across jurisdictions contributes to risks of mislabeling. While frameworks such as the International Capital Market Association's Green Bond Principles or the emerging EU Taxonomy provide guidance for sustainable finance, there is not yet a universally accepted taxonomy for nature bonds. This fragmentation allows issuers to adopt lenient definitions of eligibility, increasing the risk that bonds marketed as "nature-positive" vary widely in ambition and credibility. Investors, confronted with inconsistent standards, may struggle to differentiate between high-quality instruments and those with weak environmental underpinnings.

Disclosure practices represent another area of vulnerability. Inadequate or opaque reporting prevents investors from verifying whether funds are being used effectively. Issuers may highlight positive aspects of projects while omitting challenges, trade-offs, or failures. Selective reporting can create the impression of strong performance while concealing underperformance or unintended consequences, such as community displacement or biodiversity trade-offs. Without robust requirements for transparency, nature bonds risk becoming vehicles for public relations rather than genuine ecological improvement.

The reputational risk associated with greenwashing is significant. If high-profile issuances are revealed to have overstated or fabricated impacts, investor trust in the entire market can be damaged. Skepticism about greenwashing has already emerged in broader sustainable finance, where critics question whether ESG funds or green bonds always deliver meaningful outcomes. For nature bonds, which are still relatively new, early cases of mislabeling could slow adoption and reduce willingness among investors to allocate capital toward biodiversity-focused instruments.

Preventing greenwashing requires strong governance and independent oversight. Third-party verification and monitoring systems play a crucial role in ensuring that reported outcomes are accurate and credible. Independent auditors, environmental NGOs, and scientific institutions can validate whether ecological targets are met, reducing opportunities for issuers to exaggerate claims. Technological tools such as remote sensing, satellite imagery, and blockchain-based reporting platforms further enhance transparency by providing objective data accessible to all stakeholders.

Regulatory frameworks are also essential to addressing risks of mislabeling. Governments and financial regulators can establish clear definitions of what qualifies as a nature bond, supported by disclosure requirements and enforcement mechanisms. International coordination can help harmonize standards across markets, reducing inconsistencies and creating a level playing field. Regulatory pressure is particularly important in preventing the misuse of nature-related labels by issuers seeking to attract sustainability-minded investors without committing to rigorous outcomes.

Investor due diligence is another safeguard against greenwashing. Sophisticated investors are increasingly scrutinizing issuances to ensure alignment with international frameworks such as the Paris Agreement or the Kunming-Montreal Global Biodiversity Framework. They also assess issuers' track records, governance structures, and monitoring systems before committing capital. The growth of ESG rating agencies and sustainability indices provides additional tools for investors to differentiate between credible instruments and those at risk of mislabeling.

Mislabeling and greenwashing risks are further complicated by trade-offs between ecological and social outcomes. Projects that emphasize conservation may inadvertently create social harms if they exclude or marginalize indigenous peoples and local communities. Issuers may present projects as biodiversity-positive without disclosing these trade-offs, raising ethical concerns and reputational risks. Addressing this requires integrating social safeguards, free prior and informed consent (FPIC), and benefit-sharing mechanisms into nature bond frameworks, ensuring that ecological and social outcomes are both transparent and equitable.

As markets for nature bonds expand, managing the risks of greenwashing and mislabeling will be critical for sustaining growth and credibility. Investors must be able to trust that their capital supports meaningful conservation and restoration, issuers must commit to transparency and accountability, and regulators must establish frameworks that ensure consistency and rigor. Without these safeguards, the potential of nature bonds to mobilize capital for biodiversity could be undermined by skepticism, fragmentation, and reputational harm. Ensuring robust verification, disclosure, and governance is therefore not only a technical requirement but a fundamental condition for the legitimacy and long-term success of nature bonds.

Financial, Political, and Market Barriers

The potential of nature bonds to mobilize large-scale capital for conservation and restoration is significant, yet their expansion faces a range of financial, political, and market barriers. These obstacles shape investor confidence, issuer willingness, and the overall ability of markets to scale. Understanding these barriers is essential to designing strategies that strengthen credibility, reduce risks, and unlock broader participation.

Financial barriers are among the most immediate challenges. Conservation and ecosystem restoration projects often involve long time horizons before ecological and financial returns are visible. Investors accustomed to short- or medium-term payback periods may be reluctant to commit capital to instruments tied to decades-long outcomes such as forest growth or watershed recovery. This mismatch between ecological and financial timelines complicates structuring and pricing, making nature bonds less attractive compared to more conventional green instruments.

Another financial barrier lies in the perceived risk profile of conservation projects. Ecosystem outcomes are subject to natural variability, climate shocks, and human pressures such as illegal logging or land conversion. These uncertainties increase the risk that issuers may fail to meet ecological performance targets linked to bond repayment terms. Investors demand higher yields to compensate for such risks, raising the cost of capital for issuers. Without sufficient credit enhancements or guarantees, many nature bond projects struggle to achieve competitiveness in financial markets.

Transaction costs also pose a barrier. Designing and issuing nature bonds requires specialized expertise in both finance and ecology, as well as robust monitoring and verification systems. These costs are particularly high for small-scale projects, limiting participation by local governments, community organizations, or smaller corporations. Economies of scale are difficult to achieve without pooled structures or standardized frameworks, creating an additional hurdle for broader adoption.

Political barriers further complicate the development of nature bond markets. Conservation and restoration projects often depend on strong governance, clear land tenure, and consistent regulatory frameworks. In many countries, particularly in the Global South where biodiversity is richest, weak governance and unclear property rights undermine confidence that conservation commitments will be enforced. Investors may fear political interference, policy reversals, or corruption, which can derail projects and erode financial returns.

Policy instability is another political barrier. Changes in government priorities, budget allocations, or environmental regulations can undermine long-term commitments necessary for nature bond success. For example, a government may issue a sovereign nature bond tied to forest protection, only to later weaken environmental enforcement under political pressure. Such unpredictability raises concerns about creditworthiness and credibility, deterring investors.

Geopolitical dynamics also play a role. International cooperation is essential for addressing biodiversity loss, yet political tensions can disrupt cross-border initiatives or undermine multilateral frameworks. Disagreements over financing responsibilities, particularly between developed and developing countries, can stall progress in mobilizing resources at scale. This tension reflects broader debates over equity in global climate and biodiversity governance, influencing how nature bonds are perceived and supported internationally.

Market barriers limit the ability of nature bonds to scale into mainstream financial instruments. The market remains nascent, with relatively few issuances compared to green bonds or sustainability-linked bonds. This lack of track record reduces liquidity, making it harder for investors to enter or exit positions efficiently. Thin secondary markets discourage participation from institutional investors who require liquid instruments to manage large portfolios.

The absence of universally accepted standards and taxonomies also hampers market development. Without harmonized definitions of what qualifies as a nature bond, issuers face uncertainty in structuring instruments, and investors face difficulty comparing offerings. This fragmentation increases the risk of mislabeling and greenwashing, eroding trust in the market. Standardization is needed to create the clarity and comparability that drive liquidity and scale.

Another market barrier is the uneven distribution of demand. While there is growing interest in biodiversity finance, most investor attention remains concentrated on climate mitigation instruments such as green bonds. Energy transition projects are often perceived as more straightforward, measurable, and scalable, leaving ecosystem-focused instruments in a secondary position. This imbalance in demand makes it harder for nature bonds to compete for capital, particularly in early stages of market development.

Awareness and capacity gaps further restrict market growth. Many potential issuers, particularly in emerging markets, lack the technical knowledge to design nature bonds or the institutional capacity to implement robust monitoring and reporting. Similarly, investors may lack the expertise to assess biodiversity risks and opportunities, limiting their ability to evaluate bond structures. Without capacity building and technical assistance, the market risks remaining confined to a small group of sophisticated actors.

Currency and macroeconomic risks add another layer of complexity. Many biodiversity-rich countries face volatile currencies, inflationary pressures, or fiscal constraints. Issuing nature bonds in international markets exposes them to foreign exchange risks that can deter investors. Conversely, issuing in local currencies may limit investor pools and raise borrowing costs. These macroeconomic challenges intersect with financial and political barriers, creating compounded obstacles for market growth.

Overcoming financial, political, and market barriers requires coordinated strategies. Blended finance approaches can reduce financial risks, while guarantees and credit enhancements improve competitiveness. Political barriers can be addressed through stronger governance frameworks, clear land tenure rights, and alignment with international biodiversity commitments. Market barriers require standardization, capacity building, and deliberate efforts to enhance liquidity and comparability. By addressing these obstacles systematically, nature bonds can transition from niche innovations to mainstream tools for financing biodiversity and ecosystem resilience.

Ensuring Long-Term Environmental Impact

For nature bonds to fulfill their promise as transformative instruments in sustainable finance, they must deliver more than short-term outcomes—they must ensure durable and meaningful environmental impact. This requirement sets a high bar, as ecosystems evolve over decades and conservation benefits often depend on long-term protection, adaptive management, and continuous community engagement. Investors, issuers, and regulators alike must design frameworks that not only mobilize capital but also guarantee that the ecological benefits financed today persist well into the future.

A key aspect of ensuring long-term impact is the careful selection of projects. Not all conservation or restoration activities yield durable outcomes. Projects must be designed to address the root causes of biodiversity loss, such as deforestation, overfishing, or land degradation, rather than focusing only on superficial or temporary fixes. For example, planting monoculture forests may provide short-term carbon gains but often undermines biodiversity and resilience. Nature bonds that prioritize diverse, ecologically sound restoration approaches are more likely to sustain impact over time. This requires rigorous project appraisal processes that integrate ecological science, local knowledge, and risk assessments before issuance.

Legal and institutional safeguards are also critical to maintaining long-term outcomes. Protected areas financed through nature bonds must be backed by enforceable legal frameworks that prevent future exploitation or degradation. Similarly, restoration projects should be embedded in land tenure systems that provide security for local communities and stakeholders. Without such safeguards, investments risk being reversed when political or economic pressures shift. Strong governance structures at both national and local levels provide the continuity necessary for ecological gains to endure across political cycles and market fluctuations.

Monitoring and verification systems play a central role in sustaining environmental impact. Nature bonds typically link financial terms to ecological outcomes, but these outcomes must be tracked beyond the lifespan of the bond to ensure they remain intact. Independent monitoring using satellite imagery, biodiversity surveys, and community-based reporting can provide long-term oversight. Verification should not be a one-off exercise but a continuous process that documents progress, identifies challenges, and informs adaptive management. The integration of long-term monitoring into bond frameworks reassures investors and stakeholders that ecological benefits are maintained, not just achieved for reporting purposes.

Another pillar of lasting impact is adaptive management. Ecosystems are dynamic and subject to climate variability, invasive species, and human pressures that cannot always be predicted at the time of bond issuance. Bond frameworks should allow for flexibility in project implementation, enabling adjustments when conditions change. For instance, a reforestation project may need to shift tree species composition in response to shifting rainfall patterns. Embedding adaptive management principles ensures that investments remain relevant and effective over time, even under uncertain ecological futures.

Community engagement and empowerment are essential for maintaining long-term outcomes. Indigenous peoples and local communities are often the primary stewards of ecosystems, and their support is critical for ensuring ecological gains persist. Nature bonds can integrate benefit-sharing mechanisms, capacity-building programs, and participatory governance structures that secure community ownership of conservation initiatives. When local stakeholders derive tangible benefits—such as livelihoods, education, or healthcare—from projects, they are more likely to maintain and defend them over the long term. Conversely, projects that neglect community rights or exclude local voices risk creating conflict and undermining sustainability.

Financial sustainability beyond the bond lifecycle is another consideration. Conservation and restoration often require ongoing management, monitoring, and enforcement that extend beyond the term of the bond. Ensuring long-term financing can involve creating endowment funds, trust funds, or revolving credit facilities supported by bond proceeds. These mechanisms provide a steady flow of resources after the bond matures, preventing ecological backsliding once capital markets have moved on. Linking nature bonds with other revenue streams, such as payments for ecosystem services, carbon markets, or sustainable tourism, further enhances financial durability.

Aligning nature bonds with global frameworks also strengthens long-term impact. By linking projects to targets under the Paris Agreement or the Kunming-Montreal Global Biodiversity Framework, issuers ensure that financed activities contribute to broader, internationally recognized goals. This alignment creates continuity across political cycles, as global commitments tend to endure even when national policies shift. It also enhances accountability by situating individual bonds within a collective effort to achieve lasting ecological outcomes.

The durability of impact also depends on addressing trade-offs and unintended consequences. Conservation projects may deliver ecological benefits while creating social or economic challenges, such as restricted access to resources or displacement of communities. Long-term success requires integrating social safeguards, FPIC, and mechanisms to mitigate negative impacts. By proactively addressing these challenges, issuers reduce the risk that conflicts or inequities will undermine conservation gains in the future.

Transparency is another crucial factor. Long-term trust in nature bonds depends on open communication about successes, failures, and lessons learned. Issuers should commit to publishing detailed impact reports that extend beyond the lifetime of the bond, documenting how ecological outcomes have been sustained. Transparent reporting strengthens accountability, builds investor confidence, and supports the development of best practices for future issuances.

Finally, ensuring long-term environmental impact requires embedding resilience into bond structures. Ecosystems financed through nature bonds must be resilient not only to current threats but also to future pressures, including climate change, urbanization, and economic growth. Designing projects that enhance ecosystem adaptability—such as restoring habitat connectivity, protecting climate refugia, or integrating traditional ecological knowledge— ensures that conservation outcomes remain relevant in changing conditions. Resilient ecosystems are more likely to continue delivering biodiversity, carbon, and livelihood benefits over decades, fulfilling the long-term promise of nature bonds.

Incorporating these elements—rigorous project selection, legal safeguards, continuous monitoring, adaptive management, community engagement, financial sustainability, alignment with global frameworks, social safeguards, transparency, and ecosystem resilience—creates a framework through which nature bonds can ensure enduring impact. Without these measures, there is a risk that short-term gains will be celebrated but quickly eroded, leaving little to show for significant financial mobilization. With them, nature bonds can serve as powerful vehicles for lasting ecological transformation.

Chapter 8: Policy and Institutional Support

The successful development of nature bonds depends on the strength of policy frameworks and institutional support that guide their design, issuance, and monitoring. Governments, regulators, and international organizations play crucial roles in creating enabling environments that attract investment while ensuring ecological integrity. Policies that align with biodiversity and climate commitments provide legitimacy and direction, while institutions such as multilateral development banks, national development agencies, and civil society organizations supply technical expertise, risk mitigation, and oversight. This chapter explores how coordinated policy action and institutional backing can build trust, mobilize capital, and integrate nature bonds into sustainable finance systems.

Role of Multilateral Development Banks

MDBs occupy a pivotal role in the evolution and scaling of nature bonds. These institutions—such as the World Bank, the Asian Development Bank (ADB), the African Development Bank (AfDB), and the Inter-American Development Bank (IDB)—bridge public and private finance by providing technical assistance, risk mitigation, and credibility. Their interventions are indispensable in building trust, reducing uncertainty, and ensuring that capital flows toward projects that deliver both ecological and financial outcomes.

One of the most significant contributions of MDBs is their ability to provide credit enhancements. Nature bonds often finance projects in countries or regions where political, economic, or environmental risks are perceived to be high. MDBs can offer guarantees, insurance mechanisms, or subordinated financing that de-risks investments for private sector participants. By absorbing part of the risk, MDBs make nature bonds more attractive to institutional investors who might otherwise hesitate to enter less familiar markets. This catalytic role mobilizes private capital at scales that governments and philanthropic sources alone cannot achieve.

MDBs also contribute by setting standards and ensuring transparency. Their rigorous due diligence processes, environmental and social safeguards, and emphasis on governance provide confidence that financed projects meet high-quality benchmarks. In the context of nature bonds, MDBs can help define eligibility criteria, monitoring frameworks, and performance metrics that ensure ecological integrity. Their involvement reduces the risk of greenwashing and establishes precedents that issuers and investors can replicate, gradually creating consistent practices across markets.

Technical assistance is another dimension of MDB support. Many potential issuers—particularly in developing countries—lack the expertise to design, structure, and manage nature bonds. MDBs provide capacity-building programs, advisory services, and knowledge-sharing platforms that enable governments, municipalities, and corporations to engage in biodiversity finance. By strengthening institutional capacity, MDBs ensure that issuers can meet investor expectations, comply with monitoring requirements, and deliver measurable outcomes. Technical assistance also extends to local communities, ensuring that projects incorporate participatory governance and benefit-sharing mechanisms.

MDBs act as conveners, bringing together governments, investors, civil society, and international organizations to collaborate on financing biodiversity and conservation. Their ability to coordinate stakeholders reduces fragmentation and fosters alignment with global frameworks such as the Paris Agreement and the Kunming-Montreal Global Biodiversity Framework. Through partnerships and co-financing arrangements, MDBs help harmonize efforts across countries and sectors, ensuring that nature bonds contribute to broader sustainability agendas.

Sovereign issuance of nature bonds often relies heavily on MDB involvement. Governments in emerging markets may face limited access to international capital markets or high borrowing costs. MDBs can step in by providing co-financing, guarantees, or technical guidance that enables sovereign issuers to launch credible and competitive instruments. The presence of MDBs reassures investors about repayment capacity, policy alignment, and monitoring standards. Successful sovereign issuances can serve as benchmarks that encourage replication at sub-sovereign and corporate levels.

MDBs also play a role in integrating nature bonds into blended finance structures. Conservation projects frequently face a mismatch between the high upfront costs of restoration and the delayed realization of ecological and financial benefits. By blending concessional funds from donors with private investment, MDBs create financing structures that balance risk and return. Nature bonds within these structures can mobilize larger volumes of capital while maintaining accountability for long-term outcomes.

Another contribution lies in innovation. MDBs have historically pioneered new financial instruments, from catastrophe bonds to climate resilience funds. In the case of nature bonds, MDBs can experiment with hybrid structures that combine use-of-proceeds models with performance-linked repayment mechanisms. They can also explore digital innovations such as tokenization, blockchain-based monitoring, and data-driven verification systems. By piloting such innovations, MDBs expand the toolkit available to issuers and investors while testing models that can later be scaled globally.

Investor confidence in nature bonds is strengthened by MDB involvement. Institutional investors often seek products with clear governance, robust safeguards, and credible oversight. MDBs provide exactly this assurance by embedding rigorous standards into bond structures. Their participation signals to the market that a given issuance meets international best practices, reducing reputational risk for investors and issuers alike. This signaling function is particularly valuable in a nascent market where credibility is still being built.

MDBs also facilitate alignment between nature bonds and international climate and biodiversity commitments. By embedding GBF or NDC-related indicators into bond frameworks, MDBs ensure that financing contributes to global targets while reinforcing national commitments. This alignment strengthens policy coherence and increases the likelihood that projects financed through nature bonds deliver durable impact. MDBs' ability to integrate local projects into global agendas further enhances their relevance and legitimacy.

In many cases, MDBs also help ensure social inclusion and equity. Their safeguards and emphasis on community participation require issuers to respect indigenous rights, secure FPIC, and integrate benefit-sharing mechanisms. This reduces the risk of social conflict while strengthening the legitimacy of conservation projects. By embedding equity into financial structures, MDBs ensure that nature bonds deliver not only ecological benefits but also social resilience.

Through these multiple roles—de-risking investments, setting standards, providing technical assistance, convening stakeholders, enabling sovereign issuances, facilitating blended finance, pioneering innovation, strengthening investor confidence, aligning with global frameworks, and ensuring social inclusion—multilateral development banks are indispensable to the future of nature bonds. Their involvement ensures that these instruments grow beyond niche applications into scalable, credible, and impactful tools for financing biodiversity and ecosystem resilience.

National and Regional Policy Frameworks

The effectiveness and scalability of nature bonds depend heavily on the strength and coherence of national and regional policy frameworks. These frameworks provide the legal, regulatory, and institutional foundations that determine whether nature bonds can mobilize capital, attract investor confidence, and deliver credible ecological outcomes. Without supportive policies, nature bonds risk remaining niche instruments with limited impact. With them, they can become powerful tools for advancing national biodiversity goals and regional sustainability agendas.

At the national level, legal clarity is fundamental. Nature bonds require predictable regulatory environments that clearly define land rights, resource access, and environmental responsibilities. Secure tenure and property rights provide assurance to investors that conservation or restoration projects financed by bonds will not be undermined by disputes or weak enforcement. Governments that codify these rights create conditions where capital can flow into long-term projects with confidence. Conversely, unclear or contested legal frameworks increase risks of non-performance and discourage issuance.

Environmental regulations are another cornerstone of national policy frameworks. Strong laws that protect ecosystems, regulate resource use, and enforce conservation commitments provide credibility to projects financed through nature bonds. For example, forestry regulations that restrict deforestation or fisheries policies that enforce sustainable quotas create baselines against which bond-financed interventions can be measured. Policy consistency across ministries—environment, finance, and development—is essential to prevent fragmentation and ensure that bond-financed projects align with national priorities.

National climate and biodiversity strategies also shape the design of nature bonds. Many countries embed commitments to ecosystem restoration, reforestation, or coastal protection in their NDCs under the Paris Agreement or in their national biodiversity strategies under the Kunming-Montreal Global Biodiversity Framework. By linking nature bonds to these commitments, governments can demonstrate coherence between international obligations and domestic finance. This not only strengthens investor confidence but also provides governments with tools to achieve their policy targets.

Fiscal and financial policies can further encourage issuance. Tax incentives, subsidies, or preferential treatment for investors in nature bonds can stimulate demand and reduce borrowing costs. Central banks and financial regulators can also support by recognizing nature bonds as eligible assets in reserve requirements or collateral frameworks. Such measures create a favorable financial environment and signal government commitment to integrating biodiversity into economic planning.

Capacity building is another national policy priority. Designing and issuing nature bonds requires expertise in finance, ecology, and governance that many countries, particularly in the Global South, may lack. Governments can establish specialized agencies, technical units, or public-private partnerships to build this expertise. National development banks can also play a catalytic role, acting as intermediaries between international capital markets and local conservation projects. Policies that strengthen institutional capacity ensure that issuers are well equipped to manage nature bonds and deliver measurable outcomes.

At the regional level, cooperation among neighboring countries enhances the effectiveness of policy frameworks. Many ecosystems—such as river basins, forests, and marine areas—cross national borders, requiring coordinated approaches to conservation and restoration. Regional policy frameworks can establish shared priorities, pool resources, and harmonize monitoring standards. Bonds issued under regional agreements can finance transboundary projects, spreading risk and scaling impact. Such cooperation strengthens ecological outcomes while creating larger, more attractive instruments for investors.

Regional economic blocs play an important role in creating enabling environments. The European Union, for example, has developed a taxonomy for sustainable activities and disclosure requirements that set high standards for green and biodiversity finance. Similar initiatives in Africa, Asia, and Latin America could harmonize definitions of nature-related finance and ensure consistency across member states. Harmonized frameworks reduce the risk of fragmentation, increase comparability, and build investor confidence across regional markets.

Regional development banks further reinforce policy frameworks. Institutions such as the African Development Bank, Asian Development Bank, and Inter-American Development Bank provide technical assistance, co-financing, and policy advice that align national efforts with regional priorities. Their involvement also strengthens governance, ensuring that projects financed through nature bonds meet both local needs and regional sustainability targets.

Policy coherence between national and regional levels is essential. If national regulations conflict with regional frameworks, investors may face uncertainty that discourages participation. Aligning national biodiversity and climate strategies with regional commitments ensures that bond-financed projects are consistent across scales. This coherence also enhances accountability, as countries can report progress both domestically and regionally while contributing to global frameworks.

Social policies embedded in national and regional frameworks also influence the legitimacy of nature bonds. Indigenous and local community rights, benefit-sharing mechanisms, and participatory governance are critical components of sustainable conservation finance. Governments and regional bodies that establish policies protecting these rights provide safeguards that reduce social risks and strengthen long-term sustainability. Without such protections, projects risk generating conflict or exclusion, undermining both ecological and financial outcomes.

National and regional policy frameworks also need to address transparency and accountability. Mandatory disclosure requirements for issuers, standardized reporting on ecological outcomes, and independent verification mechanisms all contribute to credibility. Policies that establish clear penalties for misrepresentation or greenwashing reinforce accountability and build trust among investors. Regional platforms for data sharing and reporting can further enhance transparency and comparability across countries.

Through legal clarity, strong environmental regulations, integration with international commitments, fiscal incentives, capacity building, regional cooperation, and social safeguards, national and regional policy frameworks provide the foundation for credible and scalable nature bond markets. These frameworks ensure that nature bonds are not isolated financial innovations but integral components of broader biodiversity and climate strategies. By embedding nature bonds within coherent policy environments, governments and regional organizations can mobilize capital at scale while ensuring ecological integrity and social equity.

Public-Private Partnerships for Nature Bonds

Public-private partnerships (PPPs) are critical for advancing the development and scaling of nature bonds. These collaborative arrangements bring together the financial resources, expertise, and authority of public institutions with the innovation, efficiency, and capital of the private sector. Nature bonds, by design, require broad participation across governments, investors, corporations, and communities. PPPs provide the structure through which these diverse actors can align incentives, share risks, and deliver measurable ecological outcomes.

A defining feature of PPPs in the context of nature bonds is risk-sharing. Conservation and ecosystem restoration projects face multiple uncertainties, including ecological variability, political change, and long-term management costs. Public institutions can absorb a portion of these risks through guarantees, subsidies, or first-loss capital, making bond structures more attractive to private investors. In return, private actors bring additional capital and management expertise, enabling projects to scale beyond what public budgets could sustain alone. This blending of roles balances public accountability with private efficiency.

Governments play a central role in PPP arrangements by establishing enabling policy frameworks and ensuring regulatory clarity. They can provide the legal infrastructure necessary for issuing nature bonds, define conservation priorities, and align bond proceeds with national biodiversity and climate strategies. Public institutions also serve as guarantors, reducing credit risk for investors. In many cases, ministries of finance, environment, or development work alongside state-owned development banks to structure nature bonds that attract private capital. Their participation reassures investors that projects are backed by national commitments and policy support.

The private sector contributes in complementary ways. Corporations and financial institutions bring expertise in structuring and marketing bonds, managing funds, and identifying investment opportunities. Institutional investors such as pension funds and insurance companies provide large pools of capital with long-term horizons suitable for conservation finance. Corporate participation can also take the form of supply-chain alignment, where businesses invest in bonds linked to ecosystems critical for resource security. For example, food and beverage companies may support watershed restoration through nature bonds to secure long-term water supplies.

PPPs for nature bonds also create opportunities for innovation. Private actors often drive technological solutions for monitoring and verification, such as satellite imagery, blockchain-based reporting, or data analytics. When combined with the oversight and transparency requirements of public agencies, these innovations enhance accountability and credibility. Innovative financial structuring, such as performance-linked repayment terms or hybrid debt-equity models, is often pioneered within PPP frameworks, blending creativity with public oversight.

A key dimension of PPPs is the inclusion of local communities and civil society organizations. These groups are essential for ensuring that conservation and restoration projects financed by nature bonds are socially legitimate and ecologically effective. Public actors can facilitate participation through policy frameworks and safeguards, while private actors can provide training, jobs, and livelihood opportunities linked to conservation. Civil society organizations often act as intermediaries, bridging communities with financiers and ensuring accountability. By embedding inclusivity, PPPs strengthen both the social and ecological impact of nature bonds.

PPPs also facilitate access to blended finance, an essential mechanism for scaling nature bonds. Concessional capital from governments or philanthropic organizations can be combined with commercial capital from private investors to balance risks and returns. Public institutions provide the initial security and guarantees, while private investors bring in larger sums of capital once confidence is established. This layered financing structure ensures that projects with long-term ecological benefits but uncertain revenue streams can still access markets.

Transparency and accountability mechanisms within PPPs are central to maintaining investor confidence. Public institutions can set disclosure requirements, establish monitoring frameworks, and ensure compliance with international standards. Private actors can enhance these efforts by deploying advanced reporting technologies and publishing impact data. Independent third-party verification adds another layer of accountability, ensuring that both public and private partners deliver on commitments. The credibility of PPPs depends on this combination of oversight and transparency.

Another advantage of PPPs is their ability to align conservation finance with broader economic and development priorities. Governments often seek to link biodiversity protection with national development strategies, while private investors look for opportunities to balance impact with financial returns. PPPs can align these objectives by designing nature bonds that generate co-benefits such as job creation, water security, or climate resilience. For example, a bond financing mangrove restoration may enhance fisheries and tourism, benefiting both local economies and private investors.

Regional cooperation is often facilitated through PPP models. Governments within the same ecological region can collaborate with private investors and development institutions to issue regional nature bonds. Such arrangements reduce costs, spread risks, and generate larger instruments attractive to global investors. By pooling resources and harmonizing priorities, regional PPPs expand the scale and effectiveness of conservation finance.

Challenges remain in structuring PPPs effectively. Power imbalances between public and private actors can create tensions, with risks of public interests being overshadowed by profit motives. Ensuring that conservation goals remain central requires clear contractual agreements, transparent governance structures, and accountability mechanisms. Another challenge is the complexity of managing multiple stakeholders with differing priorities and capacities. Successful PPPs require strong coordination, trust-building, and clear roles and responsibilities.

Despite these challenges, PPPs remain a cornerstone for scaling nature bonds. They provide the institutional and financial arrangements necessary to align diverse stakeholders, share risks, and mobilize large-scale capital. By leveraging the strengths of both public and private sectors while ensuring community participation and ecological integrity, PPPs create an environment in which nature bonds can thrive. Through these partnerships, biodiversity protection and ecosystem restoration become not only feasible but financially viable at scale.

Chapter 9: Scaling Nature Bonds for Global Impact

For nature bonds to realize their full potential, they must expand beyond pilot projects and isolated issuances into instruments capable of mobilizing capital at a global scale. Scaling requires building liquid markets, harmonizing standards, and creating strong linkages with international climate and biodiversity frameworks. It also depends on engaging a diverse investor base, from institutional funds to retail markets, while ensuring that ecological and social safeguards remain central. This chapter explores strategies for scaling nature bonds, emphasizing innovation, collaboration, and global policy alignment as critical pathways to embedding them in mainstream sustainable finance.

Pathways to Mainstreaming Nature Bonds

Mainstreaming nature bonds requires transforming them from a niche innovation into a recognized, widely used instrument in global capital markets. This process involves building credibility, reducing barriers to entry, and embedding these instruments within the broader sustainable finance ecosystem. Several interconnected pathways can help scale nature bonds so they become a central component of financing for biodiversity and ecosystem services.

One pathway is standardization. Clear definitions, eligibility criteria, and reporting frameworks are necessary to provide consistency across issuances. Without standardized approaches, investors face uncertainty when comparing instruments, which limits demand and liquidity. Developing global taxonomies for nature bonds—similar to the frameworks that have advanced green bonds—would create comparability and trust. International institutions, regulators, and industry groups can lead this effort, ensuring that standards reflect scientific integrity and investor requirements.

Scaling also depends on the development of benchmarks and sovereign issuance. Sovereign nature bonds can serve as anchor instruments that set precedents for structure, reporting, and transparency. Large, liquid sovereign bonds create reference points for pricing and attract institutional investors, thereby strengthening confidence in the market. Once benchmarks are established, sub-sovereign and corporate issuances can align with them, expanding the market while maintaining credibility.

Blended finance represents another pathway. Conservation projects often carry risks and uncertain cash flows, deterring private investors. Public and philanthropic capital can de-risk nature bond structures by providing guarantees, subsidies, or first-loss positions. This risk-sharing lowers the cost of capital and attracts larger pools of institutional investment. Over time, as confidence grows, reliance on concessional finance can decline, creating a pathway from niche projects to mainstream market participation.

Technological innovation supports mainstreaming by improving monitoring and transparency. Tools such as satellite imagery, drones, and blockchain platforms enable real-time tracking of ecological outcomes, strengthening accountability. Investors gain confidence when outcomes are independently verifiable and accessible, reducing fears of greenwashing. Digital platforms also expand participation by making information more transparent and bonds more accessible to retail investors, further broadening the investor base.

Market education and capacity building are equally important. Many issuers, particularly in developing countries, lack experience in structuring or managing nature bonds. Technical assistance from development banks, international organizations, and specialized intermediaries can fill this gap. At the same time, investors require education on biodiversity risks and opportunities to make informed decisions. Building knowledge on both sides of the market ensures that nature bonds are designed credibly and evaluated accurately, reducing information asymmetry.

Integration with global policy frameworks strengthens the case for mainstreaming. Aligning nature bonds with the Paris Agreement and the Kunming-Montreal Global Biodiversity Framework provides legitimacy and ensures contributions to internationally recognized goals. Governments can further reinforce this alignment by embedding nature bonds into national financing strategies, demonstrating policy coherence and signaling long-term commitment to biodiversity finance.

Liquidity is another essential component of mainstreaming. Investors are more willing to participate when they can enter and exit positions easily. Creating indices, trading platforms, and exchange listings for nature bonds would improve liquidity and visibility. Financial innovation, including securitization or portfolio aggregation, can pool smaller projects into larger, tradable instruments, enhancing scale and efficiency.

PPPs provide another pathway by aligning government support with private capital and expertise. Governments can provide regulatory clarity, fiscal incentives, and guarantees, while private investors contribute capital and innovation. Collaborative structures reduce risks, strengthen governance, and ensure that bond-financed projects generate both ecological and social outcomes.

Finally, reputational trust is critical for mainstreaming. Ensuring that nature bonds deliver genuine, verifiable environmental benefits is the most effective way to build confidence. Transparency in reporting, independent verification, and adherence to rigorous standards reduce the risk of greenwashing and protect the credibility of the market. As more successful issuances demonstrate measurable outcomes, confidence will grow, attracting additional capital and reinforcing the cycle of mainstreaming.

Through these pathways—standardization, sovereign issuance, blended finance, technological innovation, capacity building, policy alignment, liquidity, public-private partnerships, and reputational trust—nature bonds can evolve from experimental instruments into a mainstream mechanism for financing biodiversity and ecosystem resilience.

Innovation in Financial Products and Technologies

Innovation in financial products and technologies is reshaping the way capital markets engage with sustainability, and it is especially relevant for the growth of nature bonds. These instruments require mechanisms that can both mobilize large-scale investment and ensure accountability for ecological outcomes. Advances in product design, digital technology, and market infrastructure are creating new opportunities to expand access, reduce risks, and strengthen transparency.

A major area of innovation lies in structuring financial products that embed ecological performance into repayment terms. Traditional green instruments often focus on the use of proceeds, but new structures tie coupon rates, principal repayment, or maturity schedules to verified environmental outcomes. For nature bonds, this could mean step-down interest rates if deforestation targets are reduced, or partial principal forgiveness if restoration milestones are achieved. These structures align financial incentives with conservation goals, turning ecological performance into a measurable component of creditworthiness.

Hybrid instruments are another innovation. Blending features of traditional bonds with sustainability-linked or revenue-backed mechanisms allows issuers to diversify risk and broaden investor appeal. For example, bonds can be linked to revenue from carbon credits, sustainable tourism, or ecosystem services, providing cash flow to service debt while delivering ecological outcomes. Similarly, blended finance instruments that combine concessional public capital with private investment reduce perceived risks and make projects in biodiversity-rich but capital-scarce regions viable.

Technological innovation enhances monitoring and verification, a cornerstone of credible nature bonds. Remote sensing, satellite imagery, drones, and geographic information systems (GIS) provide real-time data on land cover, forest health, water quality, and biodiversity indicators. These technologies enable independent verification of ecological performance, reducing reliance on issuer self-reporting. The integration of machine learning and artificial intelligence enhances the ability to process large datasets, identify trends, and detect anomalies, strengthening both transparency and accountability.

Blockchain technology introduces another layer of innovation by creating immutable, transparent records of ecological outcomes and financial transactions. Smart contracts can automate coupon adjustments or repayment terms based on verified performance data, ensuring that outcome-linked features are executed without delay or manipulation. Tokenization further expands accessibility by allowing bonds to be divided into smaller digital units, opening opportunities for retail investors to participate in biodiversity finance. These digital innovations not only reduce transaction costs but also democratize access to conservation-linked investments.

Financial innovation is also taking place through the development of new asset classes and indices. Just as green bond indices helped mainstream climate-related investments, biodiversity indices or nature bond benchmarks could create visibility and comparability for investors. Index inclusion provides liquidity and allows institutional investors to allocate capital systematically across diversified portfolios of nature-linked instruments. This development would further integrate nature bonds into mainstream sustainable finance.

Cross-sectoral financial products are another emerging frontier. Instruments that combine elements of green, blue, and nature bonds create opportunities to finance projects addressing multiple sustainability challenges simultaneously. For example, coastal restoration initiatives may deliver biodiversity, climate resilience, and carbon sequestration benefits, making them candidates for hybrid bonds that appeal to a wider range of investors. Cross-sectoral products reduce fragmentation and support holistic approaches to sustainability.

Insurance-linked innovations are also relevant. Conservation finance faces risks from natural disasters, climate variability, and political instability. Embedding insurance features into bond structures can provide protection for investors and issuers if unforeseen shocks undermine ecological performance. Catastrophe bonds, parametric insurance, and resilience-linked structures offer blueprints that can be adapted to nature bonds, ensuring that ecological risks are managed alongside financial risks.

Market infrastructure continues to evolve in ways that support innovation. Exchanges that list sustainable instruments, rating agencies that integrate biodiversity metrics, and disclosure platforms that standardize ecological reporting all strengthen the environment in which nature bonds operate. Innovations in digital platforms, including sustainability-focused marketplaces, create new channels for issuers and investors to connect, further expanding access to biodiversity finance.

Public and private actors both contribute to advancing these innovations. Multilateral development banks and governments experiment with pilot issuances, setting precedents and reducing risks for private investors. Corporations and financial institutions drive innovation in structuring, technology, and distribution. Partnerships between these actors foster experimentation and scaling, ensuring that lessons learned from early issuances inform broader market development.

The convergence of product innovation, technological advancement, and evolving market infrastructure is transforming the potential of nature bonds. By embedding ecological performance into financial design, leveraging digital tools for monitoring, expanding accessibility through tokenization, and creating diversified hybrid structures, innovations are turning biodiversity finance from a niche practice into a credible, scalable asset class. These developments position nature bonds as central instruments for mobilizing capital toward global biodiversity and climate goals.

Toward a Global Market for Nature Bonds

The development of a global market for nature bonds represents both a significant challenge and an immense opportunity. While green bonds and other sustainable finance instruments have already made strides in mobilizing capital for environmental priorities, biodiversity and ecosystem finance remain underrepresented. Building a truly global market requires aligning diverse financial systems, creating common standards, and fostering confidence across geographies. With ecosystems under pressure worldwide, the demand for scalable, credible, and liquid biodiversity-focused financial instruments is stronger than ever.

A central requirement for establishing a global market is standardization. Currently, nature bonds lack a universally recognized taxonomy or framework, leading to fragmentation and inconsistency. Investors face difficulties in assessing the comparability of bonds issued in different regions, while issuers may design structures that vary widely in rigor and scope. Internationally harmonized standards for eligibility, reporting, and verification would create a level playing field. Efforts by organizations such as the International Capital Market Association (ICMA), the TNFD, and the Convention on Biological Diversity could serve as foundations for a standardized global framework.

Sovereign issuance will play a pivotal role in anchoring global markets. When national governments issue nature bonds, they send strong signals of commitment to biodiversity and climate goals. Sovereign issuances can provide benchmark instruments that set precedents for pricing, transparency, and accountability. Large, liquid sovereign bonds also help establish reference points that smaller issuers can align with, creating consistency across markets. As seen in the case of green bonds, sovereign leadership often catalyzes corporate, municipal, and development finance participation, accelerating market growth.

Cross-border and regional cooperation will also be essential. Ecosystems often transcend national boundaries, such as river basins, forests, and marine areas, requiring collaborative financing solutions. Regional platforms for issuing pooled nature bonds can facilitate larger transactions, reduce risks, and appeal to global institutional investors. Harmonized regulatory frameworks within regions—such as the European Union's taxonomy or emerging initiatives in Africa, Asia, and Latin America—can serve as stepping stones toward broader international harmonization. By aligning regional frameworks with global standards, issuers and investors can participate more easily across jurisdictions.

Technology offers significant opportunities for building a global market. Digital platforms that provide transparent, real-time monitoring of ecological outcomes reduce the risk of greenwashing and increase investor confidence. Satellite data, drones, and remote sensing technologies enable standardized reporting regardless of geography. Blockchain and tokenization can facilitate global participation by creating secure, immutable records of performance and enabling fractional ownership of bonds. These innovations expand accessibility, lower transaction costs, and allow both institutional and retail investors to engage in biodiversity finance on a global scale.

Blended finance will be central to global expansion. Many biodiversity-rich countries face high perceived risks, weak governance, or limited fiscal space. Public and philanthropic actors, including MDBs, can provide guarantees, first-loss capital, or co-investment structures that de-risk private participation. Blended structures allow investors from developed markets to allocate capital into emerging markets with greater confidence. Over time, as track records are built and risks decline, private capital can assume a larger share of financing, expanding the scale and sustainability of global markets.

Investor demand for globally consistent instruments is growing. Institutional investors, including pension funds, insurance companies, and sovereign wealth funds, increasingly seek biodiversity-linked products that align with their ESG mandates. A global market for nature bonds would provide these investors with diversified opportunities across geographies, reducing concentration risk and enhancing portfolio resilience. Inclusion of nature bonds in global indices and benchmarks would further attract large-scale institutional investment by creating systematic allocation channels.

Regulatory cooperation is another critical enabler. National regulators must coordinate to reduce fragmentation and ensure that nature bonds issued in one jurisdiction can be recognized and traded in others. Cross-border regulatory harmonization on disclosure, verification, and eligibility criteria creates predictability and lowers transaction costs for global investors. Collaboration among securities regulators, central banks, and international financial organizations is essential for creating a coherent global marketplace.

Market liquidity must also be prioritized. For a global market to function effectively, investors need the ability to buy and sell nature bonds efficiently. Secondary market development is essential, requiring trading platforms, indices, and market makers willing to facilitate liquidity. Sovereign and large corporate issuances can anchor liquidity, while smaller issuances can align with these benchmarks to participate in broader trading ecosystems. Over time, the creation of ETFs or biodiversity indices tied to nature bonds could further deepen liquidity and attract diverse investors.

Global frameworks such as the Paris Agreement and the Kunming-Montreal Global Biodiversity Framework provide legitimacy and alignment for nature bonds. By linking bond proceeds to targets within these agreements, issuers ensure that their instruments contribute to internationally recognized goals. This alignment reduces reputational risk and increases investor confidence that capital supports globally relevant outcomes. Embedding nature bonds within these frameworks also fosters accountability, as issuers must demonstrate measurable contributions to agreed biodiversity and climate targets.

Challenges remain in creating a global market. Variability in governance quality, economic stability, and ecological conditions across countries introduces complexity. Political resistance to international coordination can slow progress, while capacity gaps in developing countries limit participation. Overcoming these challenges requires deliberate efforts to provide technical assistance, build local capacity, and foster trust among stakeholders. Strong partnerships between developed and developing countries, facilitated by MDBs and international organizations, will be key.

The pathway toward a global market for nature bonds will therefore involve multiple strategies: standardization of frameworks, sovereign leadership, regional cooperation, technological innovation, blended finance, regulatory coordination, and liquidity development. Each of these elements reinforces the others, creating conditions for scale, credibility, and accessibility.

As markets for sustainable finance continue to evolve, nature bonds represent a critical frontier for aligning financial flows with biodiversity and ecosystem priorities. By building a global market, the world can move closer to mobilizing the scale of capital required to halt and reverse ecosystem degradation. The convergence of innovation, policy alignment, and investor demand offers a timely opportunity to transform nature bonds into a central mechanism of global sustainable finance.

Conclusion

Nature bonds represent an emerging class of financial instruments that directly connect the functioning of global capital markets with the preservation and restoration of natural systems. By tying debt financing to ecological performance, they create a bridge between investor expectations for returns and society's urgent need to safeguard biodiversity, strengthen resilience, and reduce climate risks. Their design transforms natural capital from an externality often ignored by markets into a measurable and valuable component of financial decision-making.

Throughout this book, the discussion has highlighted the conceptual foundations of nature bonds, the range of financial structures available, and the institutional mechanisms required to maintain credibility. Particular attention has been given to governance, transparency, and verification, as these elements are central to preventing greenwashing and ensuring investor trust. The integration of nature bonds with international frameworks such as the Paris Agreement and the Kunming-Montreal Global Biodiversity Framework further underscores their strategic relevance in advancing global environmental goals.

The practical dimensions of scaling nature bonds were also explored, from the role of multilateral development banks in de-risking investments to the importance of public-private partnerships in mobilizing blended finance. Pathways to mainstreaming involve not only sovereign and corporate issuances but also the establishment of standardized reporting, secondary markets, and technological innovations that improve monitoring. These elements collectively contribute to transforming nature bonds from experimental instruments into liquid, credible, and widely traded products within sustainable finance.

Challenges remain substantial. Market fragmentation, inconsistent standards, and political uncertainty create barriers to scaling. Financial risks tied to ecological variability or weak governance in some jurisdictions also complicate investor participation. Moreover, without strong safeguards for indigenous peoples and local communities, there is a risk that conservation finance could reproduce inequalities rather than advance inclusive sustainability. Addressing these challenges requires coordinated policy frameworks, transparent verification mechanisms, and a commitment to equity at every stage of bond design and implementation.

Despite these hurdles, the promise of nature bonds is undeniable. They provide governments, corporations, and investors with a tangible mechanism to align financial flows with biodiversity and climate objectives. They offer a way to diversify the landscape of sustainable finance, moving beyond carbon-centered instruments toward more holistic approaches that value ecosystems in their entirety. Perhaps most importantly, they signal a paradigm shift in which ecological health is no longer peripheral to financial stability but an essential foundation for long-term prosperity.

The future of nature bonds will be shaped by innovation, policy alignment, and growing investor demand for credible sustainability-linked assets. As markets mature and frameworks solidify, their role is likely to expand, enabling capital to flow more systematically toward projects that restore ecosystems, protect biodiversity, and build resilience to climate shocks. In this way, nature bonds embody both a financial innovation and a moral imperative, offering a path toward reconciling economic growth with ecological stewardship.

www.ingramcontent.com/pod-product-compliance
Lightning Source LLC
Chambersburg PA
CBHW071606200326
41519CB00021BB/6893